"I couldn't put this book down. In ten hours I cried through a box of Kleenex, laughed out loud, inwardly smiled, felt very nauseous, became extremely angry, then was filled with awe and gratitude. *Six Years in the Hanoi Hilton* should be required reading for every high school student in the nation. It is an American treasure, but then it was written about one. I am proud to have called Jim Shively a friend and I'm proud of his daughter. Amy is a gifted writer. Kudos to her for sharing her dad's story with the world."

—Debra Wilde, former news anchor and journalist, Spokane

"*Six Years in the Hanoi Hilton* is an outstanding tribute to a remarkable person. The story of Jim Shively truly shows off the best of the human spirit. Including the brutal, heartbreaking, and heroic six years he spent as a POW, this account also captures wonderful moments from his formative years, days as a fighter pilot, father, and family man. Amy has taken an extraordinary amount of history and detail and with wonderful storytelling has presented us the life of Jim Shively with a great deal of humanness and humor."

—Ken Hopkins, program director and morning co-host of the *Dave, Ken & Molly* show at 92.9 ZZU in Spokane

"As a classmate of Jim Shively at the Air Force Academy and a lifelong friend, I am truly ecstatic that Jim's daughter, Amy, has written this book. My wife, Sandy, and I have spent many, many hours not just reading the book, but discussing it in considerable detail. I have not read any other book on the POW experience that impressed me to the same extent. I believe the reader will be greatly pleased and blessed by the absolutely wonderful rendition and research by Amy. Jim Shively was truly a gentleman and man among men, and I will never forget his terrible wounds staring us in the face each day from his heroic resistance. Obviously, by this outstanding book, it is clear his spirit, courage, and excellence remain with us on earth in his daughter, Amy, as well as with him where he is now. Thank you, Amy, this book has been a spectacular confirmation of my very highest opinion of your dear father and my dear friend. All the best to you for its wonderful success, which I believe will greatly bless our country in many, many ways."

—Captain Guy G. Gruters, motivational POW speaker and author of *Locked Up With God*

"*Six Years in the Hanoi Hilton* is not merely a story of war, captivity, and torture. It is the story of a special man, one of the best and brightest of his generation. Jim Shively's faith, inner strength, patriotism, and humility were the hallmarks of a truly great American. He was a man of character and dedication to service. It was my distinct privilege to know Jim Shively. We became friends relatively late in his life. He shared many memories, some about his captivity in Vietnam. But mostly Jim offered a perspective on life filled with a rare honesty and sincerity that made every hour with him an honor. Through the pages of this book, that honor is now yours."

—Mike Fitzsimmons, award-winning radio and television journalist, news director, and talk radio host, KXLY Newsradio 920, Spokane

"A wonderful tribute to a great man. This book is great for Vets, family or friends of Vets, and just about anyone who appreciates our servicemen. The stories in Amy's book are heartbreaking, frustrating, but also inspiring. I love Jim Shively and I love this book!"

—Dave Sposito, morning co-host of the *Dave, Ken & Molly Show* at 92.9 ZZU in Spokane

SIX YEARS IN THE HANOI HILTON

SIX YEARS IN THE HANOI HILTON

AN EXTRAORDINARY STORY OF COURAGE AND SURVIVAL IN VIETNAM

AMY SHIVELY HAWK

WITH A FOREWORD BY SENATOR JOHN McCAIN

REGNERY
HISTORY

Regnery History™ is a trademark of Salem Communications Holding Corporation; Regnery® is a registered trademark of Salem Communications Holding Corporation

Cataloging-in-Publication Data on file with the Library of Congress
ISBN 978-1-62157-510-8

Published in the United States by
Regnery History
An imprint of Regnery Publishing
A Division of Salem Media Group
300 New Jersey Ave NW
Washington, DC 20001
www.RegneryHistory.com

Manufactured in the United States of America

10 9 8 7 6 5 4 3 2 1

Books are available in quantity for promotional or premium use. For information on discounts and terms, please visit our website: www.Regnery.com.

Distributed to the trade by
Perseus Distribution
www.perseusdistribution.com

I wrote this book for Jim's grandchildren: Savanna, Cruise, Ian, Sierra, James, Ada, Anson, Elsa, and Mabel. May your Papa's legacy of courage and honor live on in you.

CONTENTS

Part Three

Author's Note

I am Jim Shively's stepdaughter. Jim married my mom when I was five, and raised me and my younger sister, Jane, as his own, so I always called him "Dad" and thought of him as such. He was a man of few words. Three days before he died he said he loved me. It was the first time I recall him saying it.

After he passed away in 2006, I learned that he had made several hours' worth of recordings about his experience as a Vietnam prisoner of war with a news reporter named Steve Becker. Steve had always been fascinated by my dad's story and felt that it should be preserved. The project took on urgency when Dad was diagnosed with prostate cancer in 2002. Following the diagnosis, he and Steve got together every Saturday for six months to record the story. This book is based on those recordings.

Listening to those CDs was the first time I had ever heard Dad talk so openly and in such detail about the war. Even when recounting his experience of torture, his deep, gravelly-from-cigarettes voice never fluctuated. He often ended his stories with a laugh. It was just how he dealt with the brutality of his experience.

Hearing his familiar voice took me straight back to my childhood, to a time when Dad read to my sisters and me, stories like *Treasure Island* and (my favorite) the entire *Little House on the Prairie* series. It's ironic that the hardships in the books he read to us were nothing compared to what he himself had endured—but we never knew until we were much older. Even then, in order to protect us, he kept most of the details to himself.

Dad loved to read. I rarely saw him without a book or a newspaper in his hand. He always hoped to write a book. I can think of no more fitting tribute to him than to capture his life and put it into words on paper the best I can.

Dad never spoke much about a personal faith, but, in my opinion, it is hard to miss the hand of God on his life. A thread of Divine Providence tied his whole life together into a thing of beauty. Providence kept him alive in the Hanoi Hilton and supplied him with grace to assimilate successfully back into civilian life. Providence turned what could have been a tragic story of despair and defeat into one of remarkable courage and victory.

I wrote this book because Captain James R. Shively was a true hero who lived a life worth remembering, worth celebrating, and worth honoring. I wrote this book to honor him and all of those brave men who withstood unthinkable sufferings for love of their country. For years, Jim Shively and his fellow POWs in Vietnam faced torture, starvation, humiliation, and deprivations most of us can hardly imagine. Their incredible service deserves to be remembered. Their story deserves to be shared with every American who values the hard-won gift of liberty we all enjoy. I am honored to write it.

Amy Shively Hawk

Special Note to POWs

To my Dad's fellow POWs in North Vietnam:

One thing I have learned while writing this book is that people remember events differently—especially when they happened more than forty years ago. I hope you will give me grace as you read, that I have done my best to stay true to my Dad's war stories as he remembered them. It is my express wish not to offend any who remember it differently. Jim Shively was not a divisive person. He valued friendship over differences of thought involving such touchy subjects as war, politics, and religion. He believed in camaraderie, loyalty, and respectfully letting others hold to their own opinion, and he taught his daughters to do the same. It is in that spirit of humility that I offer his memoir.

With highest regard,
Amy

Foreword

As prisoners of war in North Vietnam, deprived of all liberty, we relied on three things: faith in God, faith in our country, and faith in each other. Our faith in God secured our hope that we would survive. Faith in our country gave us encouragement that she would not abandon us, but would do everything possible to bring us home. And faith in each other gave us the strength we needed to get through every day. It was for each other that we did our best, despite the severity of the treatment, to resist the efforts of the enemy and to maintain our country's code of conduct. Alone we might give up, but for each other we would survive. We could not let each other down.

Reliance on those three ideologies forged within us a special unity and loyalty. Forty-two years later, those I love most and best in the world are the men I spent time with in prison. Often, we get together to reminisce about the war, comradeship, and the faith that pulled us through. It is during those times that Jim Shively is especially missed.

There is no doubt that Jim Shively was a great patriot who served both the United States Air Force and our country with a true sense of honor and courage. He was a wonderful man, a natural leader, and an exceptionally strong resistor who served his country with distinction. A man greatly respected, admired, and loved not only by his fellow POWs, but all those who knew him. Much can be learned by reading about a man with Jim Shively's level of courage and integrity. It is my pleasure to commend this tribute to his extraordinary life.

John McCain, United States Senator

Prologue

Welcome to the Hanoi Hilton

Hanoi, North Vietnam

May 1967

"Nobody asks to be a hero. Sometimes it just turns out that way."
—Staff Sergeant Matt Eversmann, *Black Hawk Down*

T he shock had worn off, and now, instead of being numb, Jim's body screamed in pain. It was the middle of the night and he was thirsty, scared, and hurting. The handcuffs were fastened so tightly they were tearing the flesh off his wrists. Blindfolded, he had no idea where he was—except that he was lying in the back of a truck, and he had no idea how long he'd been there. Dazed, he began to recall the events of the last twenty-four hours.

Flying over North Vietnam.

An explosion in the back of his plane.

The pilot behind him shouting over the radio headset, "You're on fire!"

In a sudden wave, it all came back to him. The violent expulsion from his plane, the open parachute and tranquil descent to earth, the cacophony of yelling and chaos once he landed.

He had not been prepared for the intensity of their hatred. They tried to kill him, but the armed North Vietnamese gunmen would not allow it, so they stripped and beat him instead.

The truck began moving again, and he could hear crowds of people. The yelling was getting closer and louder. Instinctively, he curled up tight in a fetal position and braced himself for more blows. The truck stopped again, but the roar of the crowd continued. Someone grabbed him under his arms and hoisted him onto a stool. Blood streamed out of his nose and into his mouth, but he couldn't wipe it because of the cuffs. They took off his blindfold. Jim blinked repeatedly in the glare of intense spotlights pointed directly at him. He shook his head to focus. A sea of North Vietnamese people surrounded him, swarming to get near. Jim squinted to see their faces. He didn't understand their words, but he could tell they were making vicious threats. Soldiers holding AK-47s lined the sidewalks, keeping the crowds at bay.

As Jim's eyes adjusted, he registered that he was strapped onto a fixed stool in the bed of a truck, wearing only his Jockey shorts. The soldiers had removed the canvas and the wooden sides from the truck, creating a moving platform from which to showcase their catch. Spotlights rigged at the top of this moving "stage" shone hotly down on Jim. The truck drove slowly through the streets of what he guessed was Hanoi. Four guards stood at each corner of the truck, their AK-47s pointed at his head. The villagers and townspeople had all come out to see the spectacle. Some ran alongside the truck. It was an enormous parade, and he was the star of the show.

A huge rock hit him in the face. The villagers began to pelt him with rocks, sticks, vegetables, and anything else handy, which he couldn't deflect because his hands were tightly cuffed behind his back. His only consolation was that the guards were being pelted too. Suddenly, a riot of angry men surged through the soldier barricade and climbed onto the truck, headed straight for him. He watched in shock as the guards used the butt ends of their AK-47s to knock them back, but there were only four guards, and the irate mob of people continued to grow in force. Jim was certain they would beat him to death on the back of the truck.

Without warning, the driver stepped on the gas, throwing everyone but Jim off the back of the truck. Jim stayed in place because his stool had been fastened somehow to the truck. The guards had to run to jump back on. This happened several times—it would even have been comical under different circumstances. Finally, after what seemed like hours, the crowds grew sparse, and they entered a quiet neighborhood.

HOA LO PRISON

He saw it from far away as they approached. The building, or rather, series of buildings, was immense. It sat on a vast, tree-lined property right in the heart of Hanoi, and from a distance it could easily have been any other governmental structure. The truck approached the main building, a whitewashed French Colonial with green shutters and louvered doors that looked like it belonged on a Hollywood set. Jim half expected some French foreign legion guy to walk out and greet him. But as the security gate opened to let them in, the compound took on a much more sinister appearance. Rows of razor wire lined the top of the buildings, along with shards of broken glass. The gate swung open to let the truck through, then slammed shut behind them with an eerie finality. He knew exactly where he was.

Built by the French in 1896 to imprison North Vietnamese rebels, the complex had been officially named "Maison Centrale," or "prison," but eventually Hoa Lo had earned itself another name: "Hell Hole." The prison lived up to its moniker. Inside its concrete walls, thousands of North Vietnamese had been stripped and crammed into dirty holding cells, sometimes twenty-five to a tiny room. Either clamped into iron stocks or chained to their bunks, they received little food or water. If not eventually beheaded, they were many times left to live in chains and die in their own excrement.

The North Vietnamese had learned about captivity, starvation, and methods of torture the hard way, and now they were putting that knowledge to use against their current enemy. Jim had heard about the prison, referred to sarcastically by the American military as the "Hanoi Hilton." No one knew for sure who had started the nickname, but a prisoner held there had once carved "Welcome to the Hanoi Hilton" on the handle of a pail by way of greeting the next "visitor." Now it was Jim's turn to be ushered into the infamous living quarters.

The guards hoisted him off the truck and strapped the blindfold back on. With his hands still tightly cuffed behind his back, they led him through a series of hallways and doors, making a big show of locking every door behind them loudly with heavy metal keys. Jim knew they wanted to intimidate him. He had the impression that they were taking him down to a basement, because it smelled musty and dirty. Eventually they entered a room where the guards took the blindfold off, set him down on a wooden stool, and left him alone. He took a look around and winced. The menacing room was all concrete—concrete floors, concrete walls, and a concrete ceiling. One dirty bulb hanging down from the ceiling provided all the light in the room—scarcely enough to see a table in the corner and iron bars and u-bolts against the wall. He looked up and noticed a hook suspended from the ceiling. A wave of fear went through him, but he pushed it aside.

To take his mind off things he decided to study the construction of the walls. Instead of smooth concrete, it looked like handfuls of plaster had been spread roughly on the walls, giving them a rough, egg-carton appearance. He wondered why they had done it that way. He found out soon enough—it was to deaden the sound.

Part One

The Making of a Fighter Pilot

HIGH FLIGHT

Oh! I have slipped the surly bonds of Earth

And danced the skies on laughter-silvered wings;

Sunward I've climbed, and joined the tumbling mirth

Of sun-split clouds,—and done a hundred things

You have not dreamed of—wheeled and soared and swung

High in the sunlit silence. Hov'ring there

I've chased the shouting wind along, and flung

my eager craft through footless halls of air.

Up, up the long, delirious, burning blue

I've topped the wind-swept heights with easy grace

Where never lark, or even eagle flew—

And, while with silent, lifting mind I've trod

The high untrespassed sanctity of space,

Put out my hand, and touched the face of God.

—John Gillespie Magee Jr.
No. 412 squadron, RCAF
(1922–1941)

Chapter 1

Baseball and BB Guns

Spokane, Washington

1953–1960

When Jim dreamed, he dreamed of baseball. He lay on his bunk in the back of the house, tossing his ball in the air and catching it, and listened to games on the radio. There he stood on a diamond in Philadelphia, pitching for the Phillies, and the announcer was calling his name. Willie Mays, Mickey Mantle, Babe Ruth, Jackie Robinson, Joe DiMaggio…and Jim Shively.

For thirteen-year-old Jim, the future was clear—and it included a top spot in the major leagues. Jim practiced at least three times a day—before school, at recess, and after school, pitching and hitting in Dishman, his Spokane, Washington, neighborhood. Dishman looked like it came straight out of a 1950s movie: idyllic rows of picture perfect homes, fronted by bright green lawns precisely trimmed. Flowers and fruit trees lined every drive. Shiny Buicks or station wagons were parked in front of each garage—one car per home. The streets were filled with kids biking, shooting marbles, and playing sports.

The Dishman grade school was just three blocks away, so Jim and his younger sister, Phyllis, rode their bikes or walked every day. More importantly for Jim with his big-time baseball aspirations, there was an empty field adjacent to the grade school. It hosted, six days a week, a work-up baseball game. The empty lot was completely void of grass and made up mostly of rocks, with bigger rocks for the bases, so the boys left every game with skinned elbows and bloody knees. Undeterred, every morning and afternoon they played, rain or shine, and also at recess.

James Richard Shively was born on March 23, 1942, in Wheeler, Texas, a tiny town just twelve miles west of the Texas-Oklahoma border. He was his parents' second son. His older brother, Harold Jr., had died, which Jim knew because he saw a picture of the grave one time, but the tragedy of his brother's loss was off-limits for discussion. Before Jim's first birthday, Harold and Jeanette picked up and moved to San Diego to join Jeanette's parents on their chicken farm. That situation did not work out, and in 1946, at the end of the war, they moved again. They made their way up north and settled in the Spokane valley.

It was a bit of an odd arrangement for those days, as Jeanette was the main breadwinner in the family. As far back as Jim could remember, she worked as a secretary and bookkeeper for the Steelworkers' Union, a position she held for more than thirty years. She left the house early in the morning and came home and made dinner at night. She ran a tight ship, and everyone knew what was expected of them. For Jim that meant keeping his room clean, doing his outside chores, making good grades, and staying out of trouble. His mom set the rules, and his dad enforced them. Harold did not take matters of discipline lightly, and so for the most part, Jim complied.

Jim's dad held a variety of jobs. He worked as a molder in an aluminum plant, a delivery guy for Sunshine Dairy, and for a while he owned and operated a Conoco gas station. Jim never knew what happened to it. But his major line of business was remodeling the Shively home. It seemed his projects were ongoing, flowing one right into the next, with the house never actually reaching completion. One day Jim came home from school to find an entire wall knocked out and a dining room where the living room used to be. When that project was complete, Harold built a garage and then connected it with a new kitchen and a different dining room. Jim's bedroom was at the back of the family home, in what had previously been a porch. His dad had closed it in and built some pine shelving and a pine bunk bed for Jim. When Harold ran out of space at ground level, he proceeded to hand-dig a basement under the house.

Harold's other preoccupation was saving money. He changed the heating system in their home frequently—from sawdust to coal, to oil, to gas, and back again, depending on what was cheapest to burn at the time. He also developed a rather ingenious method of irrigating their huge family garden, re-routing hoses in such a way that the water meter couldn't read how much water they were using. Unfortunately, he was eventually found out and had to pay a big fine to the water company.

Jim found it best to stay out of the way. He hung around outdoors with his baseball buddies, and if they weren't around he found plenty to do on the Shivelys' half-acre lot. Their backyard was home to chickens, all kinds of fruit trees, and at one time a young calf. The bountiful garden boasted enormous quantities of beans, corn, peas, beets, radishes, lettuce, potatoes, onions, and all kinds of berries. Jim loved the garden and even started a profitable business taking care of people's yards when they went on vacation. He felt sorry for Phyllis, inside doing the dishes while he mowed the grass, tended the animals, and weeded the garden, chores which earned him a dollar per week.

By the time he was twelve, Jim had caught a touch of his dad's entrepreneurial spirit. That year he answered an ad in the back of *Popular Mechanics* magazine and sent in for a Christmas variety kit. He hopped on his Schwinn, loaded down with wrapping paper, greeting cards, and various decorative items, and set off door-to-door, selling his wares to all the housewives in the neighborhood. He stood to make a great commission if he sold the whole thing, and he did.

BUSTED WITH A BB GUN

Jim and Gary rode their bikes home from sixth grade in a great deal of worry. For Jim, this was just the latest in a series of BB gun transgressions. First he had accidentally shot out the neighbor's window. Then, his friend David shot another neighbor lady in the rear while she was weeding her garden, and took off running, leaving Jim to take the blame. He had gotten out of that one by apologizing profusely and calling it, "a misfortunate accident." This latest offense was not going to be so easy to explain.

It had started innocently enough—Jim and Gary and their gang of buddies had the day off from school, so they were out tromping through the Dishman Hills with their guns. There was always something to do up there. They could make a raft out of sticks and leaves and float it on the pond. They could build a fort, shoot a squirrel, or throw rocks at a hermit tent and run away fast. On this particular day they hadn't meant to cause any trouble, but they were startled in their roaming by a group of kids they didn't know. Jim and his friends spent so much time exploring the hills that they considered them their own territory. As far as they were concerned, the other gang was trespassing. There was a small canyon dividing the two groups, and Jim and his companions had the higher ground. The Dishman gang wordlessly implemented their plan of attack, and it was a complete ambush. Within moments they had the smaller group on the ground, BB guns pointed at their heads. After a brief lecture Jim and his buddies let them go. Those guys would think twice before encroaching on their land again. Jim and his comrades-in-arms took off and forgot all about it.

All would have been well and good, except one of the victims told his dad, who happened to be head of the Spokane County Juvenile Department. Jim and his buddies got called down to the principal's office on Monday. The principal was going to call their parents, and he was giving the offending boys one day to confess before he did. Jim had a feeling this latest wrongdoing would throw his dad over the edge, so he waited until his mom got home from work to break the news. He gathered up his courage and went into the living room to face his parents as they enjoyed their after-dinner coffee. They sat quietly and listened while he confessed the whole story, and then his dad told him to go get his prized possession. Jim brought it back to him with bated breath, and watched while Harold broke it over his knee. That was the end of his BB gun.

JUNIOR HIGH

By the time Jim entered junior high, things in the little Dishman community had changed. Kids didn't roam the streets after school anymore. One of the neighbors got a TV, and the rest of the neighborhood quickly followed suit. The arrival of the television marked the end of an era. It was such a big deal that they congregated at the neighbor's house just to watch the test pattern and fiddle with the knobs. Work-up baseball couldn't compete with modern technology. Jim showed up at the baseball field with his mitt, only to find it deserted in favor of *The Mickey Mouse Club*. His dad was the last to buy a television, but when he finally did Jim and Phyllis raced home to watch *Milton Berle* like everyone else.

HIGH SCHOOL

In 1956, Jim started high school at West Valley. He was nervous at first, because Gary had moved away the summer before, so Jim didn't have a best friend. But high school turned out to be the time of his life. Not only did he excel academically, he was voted most popular and elected class president three years running, despite the fact that he spent a considerable amount of time in the vice principal's office—usually for sneaking off campus to smoke.

In 1950s fashion, the school set up a juke box in the girls' gym and let the students dance at lunch. Jim was a great dancer and a much sought-after partner. He had lots of dates, but during his senior year he dated someone special, a cute cheerleader three years his junior, named Nancy Banta.

One teacher in particular made a formidable impression on Jim: the legendary Jud Heathcote. Heathcote went on to coach Magic

Johnson at Michigan State University, including the 1979 National Championship Team, but he started his career coaching basketball and teaching geometry at West Valley High School in Spokane, Washington. He was a great coach and a gifted mathematician, but he was most famous for his outrageous temper. In the classroom, he was not above throwing chalk at students who failed to grasp key concepts, like the unfortunate basketball player who failed to understand a geometry lesson. Heathcote hurled his chalk across the room at the player, hollering, "G*@ dammit, Roger, why do you have to be such a stupid idiot?"

He was also the freshman baseball coach. Jim played baseball for Coach Heathcote his freshman year, and one game marked him forever. West Valley was competing against Lewis and Clark High School at Hart Field. It was a close game and someone had doubled, and Coach Heathcote put Jim in as a pinch runner, second base, and he got picked off at second. Coach was irate. His face turned red and he coughed and spat, unable to get his choice words out fast enough. After he had unleashed his fury, he forbade Jim to speak and moved him to the end of the bench, where Jim sat for the remainder of the season.

The real terror, though, came after the game. Coach was also the bus driver, which made for a terrifying ride when they lost the game.

By his senior year, Jim had realized he was not a great athlete. His baseball dreams had been dashed by Heathcote, so he took up as a box boy at Rosauers Supermarket, working thirty hours a week after school and on weekends. He made one dollar an hour, and what he didn't spend on cigarettes he put into savings for a car. He sacked groceries, stocked shelves, swept and dusted, and since the store couldn't sell beer or wine on Sundays, on Sunday mornings he took a big roll of butcher paper and taped it from one end of the cooler to the other to hide the alcohol.

Jim graduated in 1960 with high honors, and planned to study architecture at Montana State University. But sometime during his senior year his mom suggested he apply to the Air Force Academy, because he could get a free education there. Jim wasn't too keen on the idea, but he had been raised to be obedient. It was a very political process, and Jim relied on the fact that he probably wouldn't get an appointment.

He applied nonetheless, enduring an extensive physical exam at Fairchild Air Force Base in Spokane and a grueling fitness test at McChord Air Force Base near Tacoma. In the end, Jim came in second on Senator Henry Jackson's list of candidates. That meant he would not be going, and Jim was relieved. At the last minute, though, the number one guy withdrew his candidacy. Jim got a letter saying he had been accepted to the United States Air Force Academy. He had no desire to attend, but there was nothing he could do. He was committed.

This twist of fate would set the course for the rest of his life.

Chapter 2

"What Did I Get Myself Into?"

The Air Force Academy

Colorado Springs, Colorado

1960–1964

"**G**et your chin in!"

"Stand at attention!"

"MARCH, you son-of-a- b****!"

His "welcome" was far from welcoming. Jim hadn't known what to expect from the United States Air Force Academy, but he had not expected this. From the second he crossed the threshold, they were screaming at him.

He didn't know how to march, but no one cared. The upperclassmen in their starched khakis, white gloves, and dress hats simultaneously shouted at him and called him names. They were barking orders but he had no idea what they meant. He looked around bewildered and tried to imitate the other cadets. Somehow he managed to double-time off to the basement, where someone threw a duffle bag at him. He filed through an assembly line and filled his bag with standard issue fatigues, combat boots, and an M1 rifle. Back in the pack and clueless, he marched with the crowd, wondering where they were leading him. He found himself at the academy barber, where someone sat him down and, without a word, shaved off his hair.

DOOLIE SUMMER

As anyone who has been through the first grueling months of a U.S. military academy education knows, the training was rigorous. Every day that summer the cadets were up at 5:30, in bed at 10:00, and on the run constantly. The new cadets walked on the right side of the hall, and if they encountered upperclassmen, they were to square themselves against the wall with a respectful "By your leave, sir," waiting for permission to continue on their way. Every day consisted of military classes: instruction on assembling and disassembling the M1 and learning its various pieces, shooting at the rifle range, and drills. They pushed the limits of their physical fitness with jumping jacks, push-ups, and nonstop running.

The Air Force Academy calls its freshman "doolies," a derivative of the Greek word duolos meaning "subject" or "slave." Jim quickly learned what it meant to be a doolie, and from the first day he hated it.

Every doolie was issued a book called *Contrails*, containing important information on the Air Force Academy, the United States, and the Air Force. They were to commit to memory various points of knowledge, including every Air Force aircraft (those currently in inventory and any previous aircraft), the manufacturer, top speed, maximum altitude, number of engines, the engine manufacturer, and the armament. At any time a doolie might be asked to compare the elevation of Colorado Springs to Annapolis or West Point, or to recite General George Washington on the use of profanity during the Revolutionary War, or to quote General Spaatz about the Air Force. It was endless.

Most of the quizzing went on at mealtime, a supposedly "family-style" affair with ten people to a table. But the tables had a definite rank order. The doolies sat at the end, served the food, and ate only when the upperclassmen had taken what they wanted. Doolies served the upperclassmen at their tables, announcing the arrival of each dish: "Cadet Smith, Sir, the potatoes have arrived, Sir, would Cadet Smith or any other cadet at the table care for potatoes, Sir?" During each meal the doolies sat at attention on the front three inches of their chair, answering questions and carefully replacing their forks at a forty-five-degree angle on their plate after every bite. They were not allowed to look anywhere except down at their plates, unless someone was speaking to them. Throughout every meal, the upperclassmen would quiz them relentlessly on *Contrails*, leaving them virtually no time to eat.

The new cadets were dizzy—and not just from lack of sleep, rigorous training, and constant badgering. At 7,200 feet, the elevation in Colorado Springs took some adjustment. To make matters worse for Jim, his squadron had been assigned to the top floor. On the first day, as they ran up six flights of stairs with two bags each of heavy gear, someone in front of him passed out. Jim bent down to help him, but was curtly instructed to leave him there and run on. All he could think was, "*Good Lord, what did I get myself into?*"

It got worse at shower time. Every night the cadets endured a ritual called "shower formation," standing in line in the hall in their skivvies with a towel and a soap dish. Only five or six guys could go in to the showers at a time, so while the rest waited their turn they performed calisthenics, push-ups, and torture squats in fifteen-minute intervals. When their turn finally came, each cadet had only three minutes to shower. Coming back out they reported to the officer, "Sir, I had a bowel movement, I've checked my feet for blisters, I've showered, and I've shaved." After all that, they could finally go to bed. Taps was the only peace they had all day.

The worst came near the end of the summer. In the blistering heat, the doolies were taken into the surrounding mountains for a week of survival training. Part of the training involved learning to survive on very little food. They barely ate all week. When they returned to the academy, the doolies were welcomed with a huge steak and potatoes dinner. They positively gorged themselves. To their horror, they were ordered directly after the meal to run laps outside in the heat. Most of them, including Jim, vomited their welcome meal right back up. After that, Jim nearly threw in the towel. But he was afraid of what his parents would say and what the neighbors would think if he came home. He didn't want to let anyone down. Besides, anyone at the Academy who gave up or fell ill (or pretended to fall ill) got a double ration of hell the next day. So he pulled himself together and determined to make it through the summer, hoping that things would get better in the fall when there would be more focus on academics.

Finally, the summer ended. Later in the year, the surviving doolies were rewarded with a parade and a little propeller for their hats, (known as "Prop and Wings") signifying that they had successfully met the military training requirements and were now upperclass cadets. After that, nothing else really changed. Gradually, though, Academy life grew on Jim. He made good friends, and he and some of the other doolies even found a way to get back at the upperclassmen.

There was no shortage of good-natured harassment between the classes. Since the upperclassmen had free reign to come and go as they pleased in the doolies' rooms, Jim and his roommate rigged a bucket of water over their door, drenching their would-be harassers. Their reward for this prank came the very next day. They were quietly studying when suddenly, a huge explosion of fire came wooshing under the door. Jim shot up out of his seat as flames ignited all over the room. In a panic, the men tried to stomp out the flames while laughing upperclassmen watched from the doorway. The upperclassmen had filled a bucket with water and floated lighter fluid on top of it, throwing it under the door and scaring Jim and his roommate half to death.

That fall Jim became a boxer. He had always disliked boxing, but when the academy had trouble filling out the boxing team, they turned to the doolies, who had no choice. As much as he hated it, Jim turned out to be a natural. He was tall for his weight, and his lanky form gave him a reach on his opponents. He boxed in the 145-pound division, and much to his chagrin, Jim did so well his freshman year that he was assigned to box his second year, too.

The best part of the Academy was the above-par academic program. The professors, all military officers, were genuinely interested in their students' success. Class sizes were small, never more than fifteen students, and all classes were sectioned by academic order of merit, and re-sectioned frequently after every test. This system allowed every student to keep his own pace. It was ideal for someone like Jim, who was highly motivated to excel.

By the time his senior year rolled around, Jim had come to love the Academy. He became a squadron commander, keeping the new doolies in line. Jim also kept in touch with his favorite high school date, Nancy Banta. The two saw each other when Jim went home to Spokane on school breaks, and one time Nancy took a train out to the Academy to be his homecoming date. Jim had no idea where the romance would lead, but Nancy always held a special place in his heart.

GEORGETOWN UNIVERSITY

Jim had a particular interest in political science, and after his undergraduate studies he got into the Academy's master's program, which was in cooperation with Georgetown University. Directly upon graduation from the Academy, Jim enrolled in summer school at Georgetown, attended classes during the fall semester, wrote a thesis, and by February 1965 had a master's degree in International Relations. It was a tremendous opportunity for him and the best academic experience of his life.

That March, Jim entered pilot training. He had never considered himself a pilot and had some trepidation, but it was an expected course of action for Academy graduates. He could not have imagined where it would lead him in just a few short years.

Chapter 3

What Happens in Vegas...

Pilot Training: Williams Air Force Base, Arizona

Combat Training: Nellis Air Force Base, Nevada

1965–1966

J im sat on the ramp in his Cessna T-37 with the cockpit open, waiting for his turn to hit the runway. Clothed in heavy flying gear and a parachute pack, he was positively baking in the Arizona sun. As it turned out, he loved flying. Due to his excellent standing and graduation merit at the Air Force Academy, Jim was stationed at Williams Air Force base just outside of Phoenix, Arizona, by far the most coveted base. Before long he was promoted to first lieutenant, putting him at the same rank as most of his instructors, which made the whole experience much more relaxed and enjoyable. The daily program was split between academics and actual air time. The two squadrons rotated flight times, and Jim much preferred flying in the morning, as it was blazing hot by afternoon.

Jim was amazed at how quickly his fear turned to confidence in the air. His first plane, a little Cessna T-37 twin jet with side-by-side seating, was fully acrobatic and the only jet that could be spun on purpose and then totally recovered. He loved flying it. Still, in the learning phase of his pilot training, anything could happen.

One day early in his training, Jim was being graded on a Tech Order Climb, which meant that for every thousand feet of altitude gained, he was supposed to lose two knots of airspeed. The little Cessna was struggling, leaving Jim at a complete loss. No matter how much power he put to it, he could not maintain airspeed. Jim started to panic. The aircraft was going down. Finally, his instructor asked, "Why do you suppose you're having all this trouble?" Jim answered, "I don't know! There must be something wrong with the plane!" The instructor calmly reached over and unlocked the lever meant to stabilize the airplane when on the ground. Jim had unlocked it, but he failed to stow it properly, and it had flipped forward and locked into place during take-off. A simple mistake, yes, but Jim had no idea what would have happened if his instructor had not been there. He had to "pink" that ride: he got a pink slip and had to do it over again.

After six months and one hundred hours in the Cessna T-37, he graduated to a T-38, a much higher-performance twin-engine trainer. In the T-37 the student pilot stayed in the local area. Once in the T-38, he performed an "out and back," which meant flying to another base and back alone, with no one in a chase plane. Jim was nervous. The difficulty was not so much the flying, but multi-tasking. He had to divide his attention between flying, proper approach procedures, contacting controllers on the frequencies, and pushing the right button on the throttle to activate the radio. It took a lot of work, but he got through it.

In May 1966, after one hundred hours in the T-38, Jim graduated from pilot training and selected his airplane. The selection process was based on how the pilot ranked in the program. Jim ranked very high and put in for the ultimate supersonic aircraft, the largest single-seat, single-engine fighter-bomber in United States Air Force history: the F-105D. There were only eight assignments—and to his amazement, Jim got one.

Directly after graduation Jim started combat crew training at Nellis Air Force Base in Nevada. Of the eight pilots selected for the F-105, most were in their early twenties, and all but two were bachelors. It was a pretty great life for a hot-shot pilot: an apartment in Vegas, flying all day, and the casinos at night. Jim had no complaints.

Combat flying proved to be very different from pilot training. His earlier training had taught him the basics: rudimentary formation, acrobatics, and control of the airplane. In combat crew training the emphasis was on flying in formation, especially rejoining formations. Because bomb runs, take-offs, and landings were done individually, combat pilots had to be extremely proficient in rejoining. Jim practiced bomb delivery, strafing, and air-to-air refueling.

It was a huge jump in skill to go from flying the T-38 to the F-105. For one thing, the thrust on the bigger fighter was so strong that he had to stand on the brakes to hold it back prior to take-off. At first Jim had a hard time keeping up with the airplane. He was always two seconds behind. But before long he was flying with confidence— maybe a bit too much.

As they grew in skill, the eight fighter-pilots-in-training became infamous on base for their extreme antics. They discovered by accident one day that if they flew close enough to the water they could make rooster tails in it, just like a hydro-plane boat. This was bad news for the boaters on nearby Lake Mead. The pilots flew down the lake, barely on top of the water. Flying close to the sound barrier, with huge gusts of black smoke pouring out behind, they thought it was a riot to scare the hell out of the boaters.

They also had several misadventures, including accidentally blowing over a truck on the Nevada interstate. Jim and his buddies liked to look for "targets of opportunity" when practicing their strafing runs. Once when practicing road reconnaissance, one of the pilots scissored down the interstate, popped up, and rolled in on a truck. He got a little too low, and as he flew over the truck, the exhaust from the engine caught the flat side of the trailer and tipped it over. Fortunately, the driver was all right. Of course, nobody owned up to the incident when questioned back at the base. What happens in Vegas, stays in Vegas.

Jim's most embarrassing mishap occurred on one of his earliest solo flights. He landed long and hot (way too far down the runway, way too fast). Unable to stop in time, he took out the barrier at the end of the runway, damaging the plane and his ego. To make matters worse, his escort off the runway was General Frank Kendall Everest Jr., a.k.a. "Speedy Pete," wing commander at the 105 combat crew training. General Everest was a well-known test pilot, and famous for being one of the first people to break the sound barrier. Driving off the runway with Speedy Pete in his little staff car was the ultimate humiliation after the crash.

Another time, Jim was forced to choose life or death in an instant. He was flying Position Two in a finger four formation. The captain led them through Death Valley extremely low, about twenty feet off the ground, to make rooster tails in the sand. Without warning he turned sharply, forcing them to break formation or crash. Against all their training, they broke formation. Back at the base, the pissed-off pilots confronted the captain. The captain casually replied, "I just wanted to see what you would do."

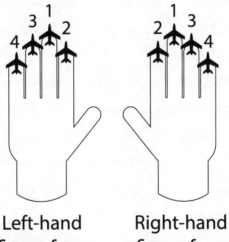

**Left-hand
finger four.**   **Right-hand
finger four.**

After recounting this incident, Jim would somberly recall the tragic 1982 Diamond Crash, involving four Thunderbirds at Davis-Monthan Air Force Base in Arizona. The four pilots in that accident had been training for an air show, and they crashed and died rather than break formation.

SECRET BASE

At the time of Jim's training there was a secret base, located just north of Las Vegas, which flew test aircraft. Of course, the pilots could see it from the air, but they had been briefed never to mention it, and under no circumstances were they to land there or use the secret base radio communication channels.

The secret base was fairly close to the gunnery range where training pilots performed strafing runs. In the F-105 a pilot could accidentally shoot himself down on a strafing run if he wasn't careful. The ricochet could hit the aircraft as it was pulling out, which happened to one of the student pilots. The F-105 sucked up a ricochet into the intake, stopping his engine. Seeing the secret base close by with its open runway, and without any other choices, he landed. The move saved him from bailing out, and it saved the plane, too. But as soon as he disembarked he was spread-eagled on the runway, searched, taken into custody, and spent the night being debriefed and questioned before they finally released him.

These were only the beginnings of the pilots' adventures. Once training ended, the pilots received their assignments. Jim's first assignment was to Southeast Asia, flying missions over North Vietnam in the aircraft with the highest losses.

Chapter 4

One Hundred Missions

Takhli Royal Thai Air Force Base, Thailand

December 1966–January 1967

I n December 1966, Jim was assigned to the 357th Tactical Fighter
Squadron at Takhli Air Base, Thailand.

Prior to taking the assignment at Takhli, he went for a week
of jungle survival training at Clark AB in the Philippines. He was
eager to fly and didn't take the survival camp too seriously. After a
few days of instruction on jungle survival skills, the airmen were
flown out in helicopters and left in the jungle in groups of twelve to
fifteen. The assignment was to learn survival skills and later, when
divided into pairs, to evade capture by the natives, called Negritos.

Jim was paired with one of his good friends from pilot training, Howie Moss, who had been an All-American linebacker at Virginia Military Institute. They were supposed to hide in the jungle for as long as possible, while the Negritos searched for them in the night. If the Negritos found them, they had to hand over their "chits," vouchers good for a bag of rice or some other prize.

Jim and Howie figured the Negritos would find them no matter how well they hid, so they decided just to kick back and relax. They smuggled in a fifth of scotch and, with the Negritos watching, found a comfortable campsite on top of the nearest hill, where there was a nice breeze and the mosquitoes wouldn't bother them too much. They even built a fire in complete violation of the point of the exercise, which was to remain in hiding. It took about ten minutes for the Negritos to raid their camp and claim their chits.

The two pilots paid for it the next morning. The drill ended with a helicopter extraction from the hiding place. The soldiers set off a flare to let the helicopter know where they were. Of course, Jim and Howie weren't too hard to find on top of their hill. The copter pilots left them there for the whole day, airlifting them out last of all.

After survival training the men were transported to Thailand and took their assignments at Takhli. The men already stationed there gave the new lieutenants a happy welcome. Mostly senior captains and majors, with some colonels, they were pleased to have some fresh blood on the wing, to replace the pilots they were losing.

Jim was an extremely good pilot and consequently became the wing man for the flight leader, Major Frank Russell, a highly regarded, level-headed pilot whom Jim greatly respected. He had flown P-47s and P-51s in World War II, been shot down more than once, and had escaped and evaded through France, hiding in haystacks. He had also flown a hundred missions in Korea and knew all about the F-105. Under Major Russell's excellent instruction, Jim grew even more confident in his combat skills.

As a fighter pilot, Jim was required to fly one hundred missions—a mark set by the Air Force, which pilots had to reach before they could return home from combat. The military didn't waste any time sending him out. He flew his first mission in December 1966. North Vietnam was divided into six target regions called "Route Packages," each of which was assigned to either the Air Force or the Navy. Route Packs were numbered I through VI, with Route Pack VI split into Pack VIA and VIB along the Northeast railroad line to China. The Air Force was responsible for operations in Route Packs I, V, and VIA. The Navy was responsible for Route Packs II, III, IV, and VIB. The highest threat Route Packs were Packs IV, V, and VI. The most dangerous area of North Vietnam was the Red River Valley, covered by Route Pack VI.

Jim's first mission was on Route Pack I, the most southern part of North Vietnam, just a few miles north of the Demilitarized Zone, the dividing line between North and South Vietnam established in 1954 at the Geneva Convention. The area had been bombed so much that it was filled with craters—Jim thought the landscape resembled the surface of the moon. There was not as much enemy warfare in this area, so it was a good place for a pilot to get his feet wet. After four or five early missions on Route Pack I, he was cleared to go anywhere, including Route Pack VI, the most dangerous area where the most airplanes were lost.

The major air targets were around Hanoi. Weather, with frequent monsoon cycles, posed a huge problem in getting to those targets. When the weather prevented them from flying north, they flew over Laos instead. Flights over Laos were conducted in cooperation with a Forward Air Controller (FAC), the person in charge of coordinating air strikes. These missions did not usually count toward a pilot's hundred missions. To get around this restriction, pilots often tried to get a "counter." If they still had gas and gun ammunition after dropping bombs in Laos, they would sometimes call back to the central air controllers for clearance to go on road reconnaissance, which meant they would fly along the roads looking for targets of opportunity. Sometimes this could make the mission count toward their one hundred.

The first time he got shot at, Jim was on a road reconnaissance mission, flying in finger four formation with three other relatively new guys. Major Russell was not flying that day. There was heavy cloud cover as they flew over the Gulf of Tonkin, screaming across the coastline into Route Pack I in search of an easy target. The North Vietnamese had been using the cloud cover to repair the road. The big construction crew with bulldozers, road graders, and big trucks made an easy target for bombing. But the pilots flew in so low and so fast that they were already over the construction crew when they saw it, so they had to circle back. That was a big mistake. By the time they returned, the road equipment had been replaced with major artillery. The North Vietnamese soldiers were ready and waiting. They opened up on them with 37 millimeters, 57 millimeters, and AK-47s. It was Jim's first time in massive enemy fire. About every fourth triple-A (Anti-Aircraft Artillery) shell was a tracer. He could see them coming, about the size of a softball, glowing red and flying right at him in a big arc. It scared the hell out of him. Without any command from the flight lead, he hit his afterburners, pulled up the nose of his plane and was through the clouds and gone as quickly as he had come in. The hot-shot pilot lost a bit of his confident edge that day.

Most missions ran about two and a half hours, longer (up to five hours) if they had to fly over the Gulf of Tonkin and across VIA and VIB. Every day they were briefed on three targets. They always planned to go to the primary target, selected in Washington. The targets were chosen as much for political purposes as for military impact. The primary target would be up around Hanoi, the secondary target in Pack V or VI, and the third would be Pack I or Pack IV. If they couldn't get any one of those three because of weather, they would go to Laos and work with the forward air controller.

In January 1967 they started going to Pack VIA more often. It was a totally different experience from flying to Laos. The skies over

6 Alpha were full of enemy fire and Soviet fighter planes, called MiGs. It was a whole new world of flying, and everyone who flew there was understandably uptight. Whenever the weather man announced in the early morning briefings that they weren't flying to Pack VI that day, the crowd would cheer. Jim always found this announcement disappointing, though. He had had his first real taste of fear, but his irrepressible quest for adventure won out. He still thought flying Pack VI was most exciting.

Chapter 5

One More Roll

In Combat

Takhli Royal Thai Air Force Base, Thailand

January–March 1967

His legs were shaking and his heart was racing in excited antici-
pation of the day ahead. It was still dark out at 5:30 a.m., and
the plane's after-burners were all lit up. Jim loved combat flying in Southeast Asia. In fact, it was the most fun he'd ever had in his
life. He loved the thrill of it, the intensity, the risk. After surviving a
few near-hits, his confidence in his ability had returned. The constant
danger didn't deplete him as it did for some pilots, it energized him.

By the time Jim came into the war in Vietnam, the Air Force had
already suffered extreme losses. He arrived in December 1966 in a new

era, with technique and strategy constantly evolving. The 357th Tactical Fighter Wing's method of combat was to come in single file at 500 feet, pop up to 1,200, then fly out at 4,500 feet. The F-105 had been designed in response to the Cold War in Europe, and it could handle high speeds, very low altitudes, and extreme weather. The only fighter with the capacity to carry a nuclear weapon in the internal bomb bay, the whole concept of the F-105 was to allow the pilot to fly in low and fast, pull the nose up, and release the bomb, which would sail miles ahead as the pilot turned and flew back the way he came, at top speed. Usually Jim exited a target area at supersonic speeds, above Mach 1.

He enjoyed the routine of it: up at 3:00 a.m. for strike briefing and intelligence, breakfast, individual flight briefing, parachute outfitting, and then gear. His gear consisted of a helmet, g-suit, vest, and a hand-held radio in case he got shot down. Once on the ramp, he completed the pre-flight check, started up the plane, and strapped in. In the States they would hook up auxiliary power units (APUs) to blow air through the engine to get it started, but over there they didn't have enough APUs. Instead they used a cartridge start, which involved pushing a button to ignite a 37-millimeter shell and the gases started the engine rolling. Jim loved the surge of adrenaline that came with sitting at the controls of this huge airplane, watching the black smoke pouring out, knowing there were bombs underneath and missiles on the wingtips.

Once the lead called check-in, he taxied down to the runway to join the other three pilots he would be flying with that day. The armament people, ready and waiting, plugged in their radios so they could talk to the pilots, checked the bombs, and pulled the pins to activate the weapons. All four planes taxied to the end of the runway and lined up. The few minutes before take-off were Jim's favorite part of the mission. His legs shook as he stood up in the cockpit, holding the huge beast back, waiting for his turn to go.

The F-105 was the biggest fighter ever built. Combat loaded, gross weight was usually fifty-three thousand pounds. One engine thrust (with burner and water) was twenty-six thousand pounds, so it took nearly the full two-mile stretch of runway to get off the ground. They took off three seconds apart. When it was his turn, Jim took his feet off the brakes and put in the afterburner, receiving a kick from the huge aircraft. Once the burner was going good he flipped the water injection and got another big boost. He had to reach regulation "go" speed by a certain distance down the runway, otherwise he would have to abort. There would not be enough runway remaining for take-off.

The rate of climb for the heavy aircraft was really slow, so as soon as he could feel the airplane come off the runway he'd pull up the gear and keep the nose down to pick up air speed. Immediately after take-off the lead began a climbing turn, and the others flew to rejoin as quickly and as crisply as possible. It was a pride thing to see which pilot could get into formation the fastest. Jim reveled in the challenge. Once they were in formation, each pilot checked the other planes visually, then usually took off their masks and lit a cigarette. It was an easy cruise out to the refueling tanker.

Just taking off and getting up to speed used up about half of their fuel, so they had to refuel quickly. The tankers floated over Laos, and each flight had an assigned tanker, which the pilots called an "anchor." The tankers were built to re-fuel slower B-52s, not F-105s, so the pilots had to stay at a very low refueling speed, around 325 knots. It was still too fast for the tanker, but that was the best match they could get.

Refueling was a challenge. It took a lot of skill just to connect to the tanker. The pilot had to pull back, slide over, put a little power on, and carefully drive up behind it. Underneath the tanker were lights and color codes, with a light that changed from red to orange to green. When the pilot got it in the green, he could connect to the boom. The F-105's refueling receptacle was right in front of the windscreen, which made it easier. The boomer would fly the plane in, and a little locking device locked it on while he took on fuel. Taking on fuel changes weight, so the pilot had to adjust lift constantly while locked on. Needing to maintain airspeed while still attached to the anchor, the pilot would have to go into a turn, changing the lift and holding altitude at 100 percent power. It got pretty hairy sometimes going around the turn at top speed while locked on, because the tanker would be dragging them around the turn. If his speed decreased the plane would disconnect, and he would have to wait until it leveled out to get back on.

The pilots took turns refueling, beginning with the lead, and then they stayed with the tanker, flying a race track pattern over Laos until it was time to be on target. As time permitted they generally cycled through the re-fueling process twice in order to have as much fuel as possible. Then the tanker put them at the north end of the anchor, and they dropped off, not far from North Vietnam.

As soon as Jim had dropped off and cleared the tanker, he did a ram-dump, which basically turned the air conditioning off and allowed for outside air to clear the cockpit of refueling fumes. Then he closed it back up and took off his mask again for another cigarette. There was usually enough time for one cigarette before he crossed the fence into North Vietnam.

As he approached North Vietnam, he did a gradual descent, coasting down to 4,500 feet. Once over the border the lead would tell them to arm their weapons. That's when things got serious. The pilots came in hot, pushing their speed up to 550 knots. They still flew in finger four formation, but instead of wingtip-to-wingtip, they spread out to about three hundred feet between each airplane, making it easier to see. Now the pilots were on the lookout for enemy MiGs, surface-to-air missiles (SAMs), and anti-aircraft artillery.

DEFENSIVE FLYING

Radio discipline was very strict once they were in North Vietnam. They had a strike frequency that was used only by the airplanes going in on a particular target. (Tankers liked to listen in, but they never said anything.) Jim used the radio only if absolutely necessary. It was important to keep quiet because once they got a few miles into North Vietnam, they would start picking up flak from the ground and get surface-to-air missile activity. His senses were on high alert, watching for enemy activity and listening for the different tones coming in on his headset. One tone alerted him to searching enemy fire, and another to enemy fire that was locked on him and tracking. The tone would change, and a light would come on, if a SAM was heading his way. A third light and a hissing sound like a rattlesnake meant they were tracking him. The rattlesnake sound really got his attention—it meant they had fired missiles that were headed straight for him. He could tell how far away the missile was by the length of an electronic arrow that came up on his tracker. The missiles were fairly easy to see, as they were about the length of a telephone pole and a little larger in diameter. They were propelled by rocket fuel, so if he was lucky he would actually see them lift off the ground in a big cloud of dust, giving him advance warning.

Major Russell explained a strategic, aggressive process for handling missiles. Whoever saw the missile first would be in control of the flight until the flight lead got it on his radar. Then they would wait, and wait, and wait until they couldn't stand it anymore, and then the lead would call brake. To call brake meant the lead would pull the stick back as far as he could and fly straight up. Number Two (which was usually Jim) would do a hard left ninety degrees, then full back stick. Number Three would turn to the right, and Four would roll upside down, so that they would all do a High-g barrel roll as quickly as possible. This aggressive maneuver was only successful if performed when the missile was in extremely close range. Since the planes were travelling at about one-third the speed of the SAM, they could turn in a shorter radius, and the SAM could not turn with them. But they had to wait until the last possible second in order for the SAM to miss them.

BOMBS AWAY

The pilots' initial point was fifteen or twenty miles away from the target. They would make their turn, put the afterburners in, and start a climb to about twelve thousand feet. At that altitude their airspeed was zero, and they could just float. Hopefully by now the target should be off to the right or left. The lead would roll-in, then plane Two, then Three, and finally Four, with a strategic space between each. They needed adequate separation between them for the bombs.

Each pilot rolled-in, got his pipper on the target, and flew straight. The pipper was a device used to predict the impact point of the bomb. At this point they weren't looking out for enemy fire, they just wanted to "put the bomb on the target." At this time there were no smart bombs, and the method of delivery was far from sophisticated. They knew temperature and winds from the early morning briefing, and what kind of bombs they were dropping, but each pilot did his own constant calculation for airspeed, altitude, and how many degrees were needed. They had to be their own computers, constantly figuring out what was needed to get their bombs on the target. Once they dropped a bomb, they needed to get as much speed as possible as quickly as possible. If the speed brakes were out, they came in. If the plane was not already in afterburner, they got it into burner and then it was, according to Jim, "keep your nose down, do a hard turn, and keep maximum g on the airplane." It was the most intense, dangerous part of the mission. Lead would have come off the target and done a big turn, so it was all about getting rejoined as quickly as possible— and "getting the hell out of there."

The airplane was going at top speed, which made turning dangerous. The pilot had to be incredibly careful. If he pulled too hard he might "swap ends" and accidentally reverse attitude, going from nose down to tail down, headed for the ground.

When he first started flying, Jim worried that he might break his airplane, but he soon learned that there is no such thing as a gentle turn in combat. A pilot had to throw the stick full left, full right, full back, jerking the plane all over the place at top speed. Facing the nonstop threat of flak and missiles, Jim flew violently and put all kinds of g's on the airplane. Upon rejoin, the pilots flew to about 4,500 feet, got out of the high-threat area, and visually checked the other planes to be sure no one was hit and everyone was okay. Every once in a while, there would be a bomb hung on the rack. In that case it had to be jettisoned off, rack and all. Then it was back to the tanker to refuel, and back to base.

One time Jim took a hit on his stabilator. He could still control the plane, but it was burning fuel at an extremely high rate. Jim knew he didn't have much time before he went down. He called the tanker and told them what his problem was. The tanker left his anchor (in violation of the rules) and met Jim in the air. Had the tanker not done that, Jim would have had to eject—he would have run out of fuel in midair.

Back at the base, about 8 a.m., they debriefed, ate a second breakfast, and napped until early afternoon. The mission for the next day would have come in by then, so they would go to Wing Operations and flight plan for the next day. When that was done, usually about 4:00, Jim took a swim in the pool or played racquetball. Then he'd have dinner and meet his buddies in the stag bar to hang out until 10 or 11 when he went to bed. The next morning at 3:00 he was up to do it all over again.

That was the standard routine, and Jim thrived on the excitement of it all. He flew just about every day. Because they were stationed in Thailand and not Vietnam, they were technically not in a combat zone, so there was no traditional R & R. Most squadrons were on duty twenty-five straight days, and then they got five days off. That didn't mean one pilot flew all twenty-five days, though. They took turns in the tower, on the runway. And occasionally they had to "sit spare" as the fifth man. There were always five airplanes fueled and ready to go, but only four took off. The fifth would sit on the runway prepared, just in case one of the four had to abort for some reason. Then the spare would take off and fly fast to catch up. Jim hated that particular duty, because it usually meant sitting on the ramp all day in the heat with the engine running. He much preferred to be in the air.

If he was not scheduled to fly or to sit spare, he sometimes did the flight planning. The targets were selected in Washington, transmitted to Saigon, and a T-39 flew target information into the base every afternoon. It was all in code, so the intelligence guys would have to break the code, and then they would plan the flight for the next day.

GOOD TIMES IN BANGKOK

Jim could do whatever he wanted for his five days off. Sometimes he and his fellow airmen took the train into Bangkok, only one hundred miles away. There they would catch the Chaing Mai Express which came through Takhli.

The American GIs were the biggest thing happening in the little town of Takhli, so whenever the pilots went off base they were swarmed. Children ran to them begging for money, trying to carry their bags, and so on. The busy train depot was chaos for the mobbed pilots, but eventually they managed to work their way through the multitudes and get on the train, a steam locomotive with wooden seats, open windows, and little fans on the ceiling. There was a dining car with an open wok where they could order a Singha beer and fried rice as they watched the countryside go by.

Literally hundreds of cabs lined the streets of Bangkok, and they all wanted the pilots' business. Now the negotiations began.

For a carton of cigarettes and a fifth of Gordon's gin per day, they could get a car and driver at their twenty-four-hour disposal for the whole week. It was a good deal for Jim and his buddies because they could buy the stuff on base for cheap. On one occasion they couldn't get Gordon's so they brought another kind, but the driver wouldn't take it. It was Gordon's or nothing, so they had to pay extra that time.

They had good times in Bangkok. Everything was inexpensive, and they spent afternoons at the swimming pool, nights out at the bars, and ate wonderful meals. Their favorite restaurant was called Nick's Number One, and they found it by accident down a hidden alley. The owner was Hungarian and served the best food Jim had ever tasted—thick goulash with huge chunks of lamb, rich potato dumplings, and spicy apple strudel.

They stayed at the Siam Intercontinental Hotel. It was new, and the flight crews stayed there, so there was always the possibility of running into stewardesses at the swimming pool. They usually stuck to the same routine: eat, drink, try to pick up girls, and sleep well into mid-morning. They visited the palace, the emerald Buddha, the golden Buddha, and a snake farm. Perhaps the most memorable sight-seeing tour landed them at a Thai boxing match. The event was interactive. Rather than sit and watch, the audience participated. Men took bets throughout the match, gambling and screaming at each other, and, through the ebb and flow of the fight, throwing punches themselves. Jim and the others were lucky to get away unharmed.

"SEE YA AROUND, BABE"

By spring of 1967, the weather turned and the pilots flew north to the more dangerous areas more frequently. There was intense pressure to count missions. In fact, the Air Force and the Navy were competing for number of missions. Even when they knew the weather would be bad, they headed for their primary target on almost every mission. At a certain point, if the weather had not improved by the time they got there, the mission commander would call the code word for weather abort, and then determine if they should fly to the first, second, or third alternate.

Pressure mounted as they put their lives at risk for their country, and for each other, daily. The men had a strong commitment to each other. Fear had no place now. No one wanted to look like he couldn't do it, but some pilots were not as courageous under fire as was expected. Everyone knew who they were. Their peers referred to them as "dip-bombers" because they somehow managed to drop their bombs from eleven thousand feet or higher. They could always claim a malfunction later, but everyone knew it was because they were afraid of being hit. One guy they nicknamed "Shaky Ray"[1] because he always managed to have some sort of aircraft problem when it was his turn to fly Route Pack VI.

Sometimes they flew when they shouldn't have. By March 1967, they had been sitting on their primary target, a steel mill complex thirty miles north of Hanoi, for weeks. The weather kept putting them off. Finally, on March 11, the wing commander announced, "Regardless of weather, we are going to make a real effort to go to this target *today*, because if we don't get on it today, the Navy's A-6s are going to get it tonight."

Jim had never flown in clouds that were so black and thick. They had to tuck in really tightly and fly in extremely close formation. If they got even five feet apart, they lost sight of each other. When they made it to the refueling tanker over Laos, it was so black that they could not see it. The tankers had to drop down below the clouds, which was a huge risk for everyone.

On this dark, cloudy day, refueling was even more difficult than usual. It required an almost minute movement of the throttle, making it an extremely tense situation for both the pilots and the tanker. If a pilot pulled back too far from the tanker, he would be lost in the clouds. Number Four in Jim's flight came off the tanker with a little too much power and disappeared into the clouds, unable to get back on formation. Major Russell commanded him to fly home alone, a huge violation of the rules under normal circumstances. Ordinarily, he would have sent Number Three back with him for safety, but not this time. The wing commander had made it clear that the mission was top priority.

They were down to three ships in terrible weather. Jim had never flown in such dangerous conditions; there were continual sound indications of missiles and anti-aircraft fire, but flying blind in a black sky, they had no visuals to guide them. Jim kept expecting the lead to call "abort," but he never did. They pressed on. Finally, they broke through the clouds, well into North Vietnam and north of the target, much lower than they liked to be. The lead flight called that the cloud cover had lifted over the target and they were going in.

They were about ten minutes behind the flight ahead of them, and Jim could tell by the radio chatter that it was a horrible day. The gunners were locked on and giving the pilots a rough time. As they approached, they heard over the radio that someone from the flight ahead of them had been shot down. They went in anyway, in three formation, with Major Russell in the middle, Jim to his right, and pilot Number Three, Captain Joseph Karins, to his left.

It came out of nowhere. A radar tracking gun was tracking Jim, and the missile was moving in fast. Major Russell radioed him and told him to move across the formation to switch places with Joe. Jim and Joe switched quickly, hoping to disrupt the enemy's ability to lock onto him.

As they reached roll-in altitude, the air around them swarmed with flak and missiles. Major Russell rolled in, then Joe after a count of three, then Jim. He was three-quarters of the way down the bomb run when a surface-to-air missile went whizzing by him and exploded into Joe's aircraft. Immediately the canopy of Joe's plane popped off. He radioed to Jim, "I'm getting out. I'll see ya around, babe." Jim watched in shock as his partner parachuted out and disappeared. The eeriness of those moments was only heightened when Joe's aircraft, which had been trimmed to a certain speed and attitude, came out of its dive and continued to fly alongside Jim's plane for several miles.

Joe and Jim flew along side by side, Joe's empty cockpit a stark reminder of what had just taken place. Joe's final farewell, "I'll see ya around, babe..." rang in Jim's ears. Finally, Joe's plane rolled over on its wing and went down.

Jim whispered, "Goodbye."

Captain Joe Karins was never accounted for. He went out at high speed directly over the target, in the middle of intense fire, so it was surmised that he was shot while still in his parachute. Jim would later receive the Distinguished Flying Cross for flying back into the extremely hostile area to pinpoint the exact position where Joe was downed, and for initiating rescue procedures.[2]

Jim had a hard time with Joe's death. Throughout his entire life, Jim never forgot that he should have been in Joe's place. He also never forgot the response of the wing commander. During debriefing, the wing commander said only, "Too bad about Joe. Did he get his bombs on the target?" Needless to say, Jim lost all respect for that wing commander. Altogether, they lost two airplanes and two pilots, and another aircraft was badly damaged—all so they could show up the Navy. To add insult to injury, the target held little value. The whole mission had been mostly for show.

The atmosphere at the squadron grew more tense and anxious by the day, as more and more pilots were downed. Depending on the location of a downed pilot, there might be rescue efforts. That meant someone from the wing might be involved in the rescue mission, protecting against MiGs and enemy fire, and providing air cover when the helicopters got there. Sometimes they had to use the guns to strafe enemy troops on the ground who might be approaching the downed pilot. Back at the wing, they waited for the report, and there was always a big celebration when a pilot was recovered. Sadly, those occasions were few and far between.

Still, Jim was hopeful. Since they were flying dangerous missions daily, his "counters" were increasing fast. He calculated that he had about a month left to serve before he reached his one hundred. Instead, his sixty-ninth mission would be his last.

Chapter 6

Shot Down

North Vietnam

May 5, 1967

May 5, 1967, was a pivotal day in combat. Washington decided to escalate the war by adding an element of surprise: for the first time they were going to hit targets right in Hanoi. In fact, Takhli was joining forces with Korat Air Force Base, another base in Thailand. Normally the F-105s out of Korat kept their targets separate, but on this strategic day they were going to hit Hanoi at the same time. The instructions from Washington were more detailed than usual, including which direction the pilots were to fly in and out. The orders were far more dangerous than anything the pilots would normally have flown.

The monsoon cycle had changed, and the weather over North Vietnam was good. They had been going north most every day, and losing air craft steadily as a result. A few days before the 357th Squadron had lost their most experienced Wild Weasel crew. This was the Air Force code name for a dedicated anti-SAM aircraft, whose mission was to destroy enemy radars and take out the SAM sites. Jim's friend Bob Abbott from pilot training at Nellis had been downed and likely captured. The mood at the base was somber.

For Jim, the mission felt bad from the start. Not only was it excessively dangerous, but he was flying with a new lead. Major Russell had reached his one hundred and gone home, and Jim missed flying with him. He had flown with this new lead a few times before, but he had not yet established the same level of confidence in him as he had in Major Russell. Jim's flight was assigned to flak suppression, which meant they would be dropping CBU-2 "cluster bombs" from an extremely low altitude. He had a bad feeling about this one.

The weather was good, and they were the first flight on the target. As they entered the target zone, they encountered an unusual amount of enemy fire. MiGs were up, SAMS were firing all around, and the flak was intense. Tracers were in the air everywhere. Only every fifth or sixth shot is a tracer, so Jim knew that enemy fire must be much worse than normal. The other shots could not be seen until they exploded, and explosions were going off all around him.

"YOU'RE ON FIRE!"

Everything was fine coming down the bomb run and off the target. He had his afterburner in and he saw the lead. But as he cut off to get back to the lead, WHAM! There was a huge explosion behind him. The nose of his airplane went straight up, then straight down. Then, instantaneously, the plane straightened itself out. Jim knew he had been hit, but he couldn't see any damage. He figured he could make it back to base. Suddenly every warning light in the plane came on, and the RPMs started winding back to zero. The engine was shutting down. He tried to restart it, with no luck. His stomach turned over.

"You're on fire!" the pilot behind him shouted into the radio. Jim tried to turn the plane around, hoping he could make it to the gulf where he was more likely to be picked up. But his airplane rebelled. As long as he kept his hands off the stick, it flew straight and level, but if he touched the stick, it went crazy. He decided to keep his hands off and stay with the plane as long as possible. He knew if he landed in the flats around Hanoi, the Air Force wouldn't even try to rescue him. His last hope was to get to the mountains west of Hanoi, but the plane was rapidly losing air speed and altitude.

To his surprise he remained quite mellow, able to think clearly. He thought, "Do I really want to get out?" He knew if he punched out, the North Vietnamese would get him, and he didn't know what they would do to him. If he stayed in the airplane, it would be over quickly.

He never made a conscious decision. His survival instinct kicked in. He pulled up the handles on his seat, blowing the canopy off the plane, then squeezed the trigger, blowing himself out of the airplane. The seat automatically separated from him and the parachute opened up, but he didn't remember it. The instantaneous g-force knocked him out. By the time he regained consciousness, he was in the air.

He woke up just in time to see his airplane hit the ground and explode. Although his mind was calm, his physical senses came alive at the same time he did—he was acutely sensitive and alert. The world was unbearably loud. In the quiet of the cockpit, all he heard were radio transmissions. He had seen, but never actually heard, the enemy fire. Now that he was out in the midst of it, the noise was deafening. Ear-piercing bombs went off in every direction, the *rat-a-tat-tat* of the anti-aircraft artillery rang out endlessly, and shrike missiles were screaming all around him. He saw a village in the distance, and people shooting upwards. He didn't know if they were shooting at him or not. A brilliant green field lay next to the village, in stark contrast to its dusty chaos. Like a glistening emerald, bathed in the golden light of the sun, it beckoned him. A strange peace came over him as he floated calmly earthward, intent on the gleaming emerald field below.

Suddenly, an F-105 whizzed past, interrupting his peaceful state. Seeing it, Jim had an abrupt, maddening thought. Gordon Jenkins, his roommate back at the wing, was in one of the planes that had just gone by. Jim felt an odd rush of fury, thinking about Gordy going off to the bars in Bangkok the next day. They were always trying to impress stewardesses with tales of their dangerous missions, and he worried that Gordy would try to score some chicks at Jim's expense. "Remember that pilot, Jim Shively? He got shot down yesterday."

In truth, Gordy did not go off to the bars the next day to brag about his successful mission. Instead he packed up Jim's belongings and sent them home with a letter of condolence to the Shively family. Gordy himself later said, "The hardest thing I ever had to do in my life was pack up his things and write a letter to his mother."[1]

With a thud, Jim landed right in the middle of the green rice paddy he had been admiring, which wasn't as pretty close up. Thankfully, it was flooded with water and made for a nice soft landing. But the force of the fall inserted him chest-deep in a thick rice-mud mixture, making it extremely difficult to move. It was like being trapped in quicksand, and although he squirmed and thrashed about to try to extricate himself, he got nowhere fast. Then he noticed a lot of red mixing with the green of the field. Both of his arms were gushing blood—he must have been injured during expulsion. He was still in a daze, but alert enough to realize that bleeding profusely and being mired in mud and rice put him at an extreme disadvantage in alluding capture. He managed to raise his injured arms above his head and struggle out of his heavy parachute. Once he had the parachute off, he twisted and turned and wiggled until the swamp was around his knees. He knew where the village was, so he headed in the opposite direction as fast as he possibly could—not very fast at all, with his heavy g-suit and survival vest, loaded with two hand-held radios, a flare pistol, flares, a .38, ammunition, and water bottles. His heart was pounding out of his chest, and he just kept thinking, "I gotta get out of here." The noise of the air raid began to dissipate, which made Jim even more nervous. Now they would be coming after him.

The quiet in the air was almost as deafening as the earlier noise had been. He could sense his followers moving closer as he waded on. Realizing he was leaving a trail, he decided to stop moving. He got down low right where he was, hoping the quiet voices would go on by. But they didn't. The people of the village descended upon him, suddenly, surrounding him on every side, a mass of hatred bearing down on him. They shouted and struck him with rakes and sticks and various farm implements. Jim covered his head with his bloody arms. He had the strange sensation of being in his chute again, looking down and watching this beating happen to someone else.

Four men stood out distinctly, wearing shorts and uniform shirts and carrying AK-47s. These four kept the others from killing him. They stripped him down to his undershorts, blindfolded him, and tied his hands tightly behind his back. All Jim could think was that he was alive, and that he should have removed the two hand-held radios from his vest and broken off the antennas before they captured him. Now it was too late.

He was sweating profusely as they led him out of the paddy and onto a road. It was afternoon, severely hot, and he was sticky with mud and rice. The villagers continued to say things and poke at him, but no one spoke English. They were marching him toward the village, a primitive community made up of nothing but straw huts. They entered one of the huts and sat him down on a stool. When they took the blindfold off, Jim realized he was on display. The local villagers paraded by to glare through the window and jeer at the captured American "air pirate."

Jim watched them go by without regard. By now he had one thing on his mind and one thing only: water. The bottles of water that had been stuffed in his g-suit had been confiscated, and he wanted them back. Additionally, his arms were still dripping blood. They didn't hurt yet, he was still numb and in shock, but he clearly needed stitches in several places. Eventually an elderly North Vietnamese woman came in and wrapped cloths around each arm. Almost immediately, they became soaked through with blood, but Jim was too thirsty to care. He could only feel the tight squeezing in his dry throat. He wished the lady would bring some water, but she never came back, and Jim sat parched and quiet while the villagers filed by one by one to have a look at him, spitting and slinging abuse through the window.

Finally, the four armed soldiers blindfolded him again and led him out of the hut. Jim guessed that they led him to a bigger road, because a truck came along and stopped, and he got passed off to the guys in the truck. They threw him in the back, where Jim lay in his underwear, handcuffed and blindfolded. Occasionally the truck would stop, either at villages or at anti-aircraft sites. When it did, the guards would take the canvas off the truck, yank him out and stand him up for all the villagers to see. They would get out their blow horn and shout, presumably to make a show of the bloody American pilot now in their possession.

At one of those stops, the North Vietnamese soldiers had put the canvas back on the truck and were getting ready to leave. Jim lay in the back, blindfolded, and a Russian man asked him if he spoke Russian. Jim had taken a year of Russian at the Air Force Academy, so he understood a little. Jim needed water badly. He could not remember for the life of him what the word for "water" was, and the man left before Jim could get his request out.

It was late at night when they made it to Hanoi. No one had spoken to him in English yet, so Jim was surprised when someone came and sat him up on the stool and asked him in English which airplane he flew. The U.S. Military Code of Conduct states that a captured officer shall only give the enemy his or her name, rank, service number, and date of birth. This policy is commonly referred to as "the big four and nothing more." As per his military training, Jim responded with his name, rank, service number, and date of birth. The North Vietnamese officer didn't like that. He retaliated by punching Jim in the nose. "With that kind of attitude," he threatened, "you're going to die." Jim, still blindfolded, had been unprepared for the punch. It pissed him off and his adrenaline kicked in, but with his hands tightly bound behind his back, he had no way to retaliate. He lay in the back of the truck where the blow had landed him, broken and bleeding.

Part Two

In Captivity

AIRMAN'S CREED

I am an American Airman.

I am a warrior.

I have answered my nation's call.

I am an American Airman.

My mission is to fly, fight, and win.

I am faithful to a proud heritage,

a tradition of honor,

and a legacy of valor.

I am an American Airman,

guardian of freedom and justice,

my nation's sword and shield,

its sentry and avenger.

I defend my country with my life.

I am an American Airman:

wingman, leader, warrior.

I will never leave an Airman behind,

I will never falter,

and I will not fail.

Chapter 7

Heartbreak Hotel

Hanoi, North Vietnam

May–July 1967

"What lies behind us and what lies before us are tiny matters compared to what lies within us."

—Ralph Waldo Emerson

Jim sat on a hard stool in the torture room at the Hanoi Hilton, staring out the window. He was hungry, but even worse was the thirst. It had been a couple days now, and all he could think about was water. He had no saliva and could feel himself becoming lethargic. He was sweating like a pig in the unbearable heat, although he still wore nothing but his jockey shorts, and the mosquitoes were eating him alive. He couldn't swat at them because his hands remained tied behind his back. He tried to focus all of his attention on not falling off the stool.

Two North Vietnamese officials came into the room, dressed in crisp uniforms with black leather jackets. They began questioning him immediately. One spoke very good English, and the other didn't, but Jim got the impression that the one who didn't was the boss. They bombarded him, unmoved by his physical condition: What was his name, rank, service number? What was his date of birth? What airplane had he been flying? Jim stuck with the code, answering the first four questions only. The North Vietnamese boss was irate. He launched into a tirade in broken English, riddled with profanities, threatening the captured "air pirate" with punishment for refusal to comply with the prison camp's rules.

Jim calmly replied that he was asserting his rights under the Geneva Convention, which required only that he provide his name, rank, service number, and date of birth. That response earned him another long lecture. The officials informed him that neither the United States nor North Vietnam had ever officially declared war, therefore the two nations were not at war and the Geneva Convention did not apply. Additionally, according to the officials, North Vietnam had never signed the Geneva Convention and was not bound by it. They claimed the United States was wantonly attacking North Vietnam. Jim was nothing but a war criminal, and he would eventually be tried, but they refused to treat him as a military officer. They never used the word "torture," but they gave him to understand that his welfare would depend on how well he cooperated with the rules of the camp. To begin with, he must answer their questions.

Weak and dizzy from lack of food and water, Jim thought their arguments made some sense. The North Vietnamese had not declared war on America, and America had not declared war on North Vietnam. From their point of view, Jim supposed he *was* a war criminal. Still, he stuck to his training. "I still have my duties and responsibilities to my job, and I cannot tell you anything except my name, rank, service number and date of birth." The official replied, "I'm sorry you have that attitude because now you'll have to be punished." They left the room. Jim sat there for a long time wondering what would happen next.

Several more hours went by. Eventually, five men entered the room, obviously much lower in rank then the two who had been there before. They immediately knocked him off the stool. Their methods were far from sophisticated: they punched him and kicked him around the floor, while he remained helpless with his hands cuffed behind his back. Afterwards, they rolled him into a sitting position on the floor. They spread his legs out in front of him as far as they would go, fixed a U-bolt on each ankle, and slid a big iron bar between them, locking them into place. Leaving his hands tied behind his back, they took another rope and tied his upper arms together tightly. Another rope was tied to the one around his upper arms, wound around his neck, and then tied to the iron bar holding his legs. They pulled it as tight as it would go so that his head was down between his legs, his arms held unnaturally in the air behind him. If he tried to move, it put pressure on the bar, twisting his ankles the wrong way.

It was the infamous "ropes" torture.

It hurt a lot. Jim lost all circulation in his arms and legs. First his limbs went to sleep, then it felt like hot needles were puncturing his flesh. After many hours, Jim realized they planned to leave him there until he gave up. All but one of the torturers had left the room. The remaining guard would periodically knock him around a little bit, but mostly he just sat and watched him. Desperate, Jim tried to knock himself out by dashing his head against the floor, but he only succeeded in hurting his head. Holding his breath didn't work either. He decided to count to one hundred. "Then," he said to himself, "I'll give up." He ended up counting one hundred over and over again, each time thinking, "Well, I can do it one more time."

Eventually he knew he couldn't take it anymore. He shouted at the guard that he gave up. But the guy didn't understand English and must have thought Jim was being smart, because instead of untying him, he started beating Jim around again. This happened several times, with Jim crying for help and the guy beating him up instead. Finally, the guy left the room. Jim hoped beyond hope that he had gone to get someone in charge, but no one came. By now he was in agony. The counting to one hundred trick wasn't working anymore. As he waited he told himself angrily, "You gave up too soon. You thought you couldn't go any longer, but you obviously could because you're still here..."

Hours went by, until a sliver of daylight found its way through the window. Finally, two men walked into the room.

"Are you ready to answer the questions now?" they asked.

Jim was. They untied him, but for a long while he felt no relief. The loss of circulation to his limbs left him paralyzed, every limb completely numb. His questioners barked at him to get off the floor and sit on the stool, but he could not move. He lay humiliated and helpless on the floor, like a fish. Finally, he managed to maneuver himself back onto the stool. They wasted no time on formalities, but picked right back up where they had left off. What airplane had he flown?

"I can't talk…I need water," he croaked, using one of the techniques he learned in survival school training in an attempt to stall them. Apparently they had been through the same training. The men replied, "After you answer the questions, you'll get water." They replayed that scene a couple more times, and then they reached for the ropes. Jim knew he couldn't go through that again. He answered reluctantly, "An F-105," which of course they already knew, because the villagers had told them.

They asked him what tomorrow's targets would be. Jim told them he didn't know. What did he think the targets would be? Jim rattled off targets the U.S. had already bombed, which really pissed them off. They reverted to questions about information they already knew, like the altitude he flew in at. Finally, they left, without giving him any water. By now it had been several days.

Jim lost all track of time. He kept falling asleep and slipping off the stool onto the concrete floor, waking himself up with a jolt. His dignity demanded that he get back up on the stool again each time he fell off, although it was very difficult in his dehydrated, feverish state, with his hands still tied behind his back, and the cuts in his arms becoming grossly infected. He did not want them to find him on the floor when they came back. He didn't know how much longer he could survive without water. As the hours passed, the fever grew steadily worse until he lost consciousness. This time when he fell off the stool he didn't get up until a guard came in and kicked him awake. This happened a few more times until someone finally brought him some water.

He revived enough to notice that at some point when he had lost consciousness, they had removed the handcuffs and untied his upper arms. He stared at his forearms in disbelief. They had swelled to twice their normal size, like a hideous Popeye. The bandages that the old lady had tied on him were still in place, but they were filthy with dried blood, dirt, and pus. Jim unwrapped his arms slowly, squeezing out the pus. The drainage was a huge relief, but his arms soon swelled again.

They left him there for several days. Starvation, fever, and dehydration made him lose consciousness several times, and he would remain passed out on the floor until a guard kicked him awake. Then he would get back on the stool and squeeze the pus out of his swollen arms. They offered him no food, and water only sparingly, barely enough to keep him alive. He didn't know how things could get any worse—until they did.

ISOLATION

The next time he woke up, they had him in another room, even worse than the first. He had no idea how he got there—or what he'd done to deserve it. He learned later that the prisoners called this part of the prison Heartbreak Hotel.

It was a tiny concrete cell, barely six feet by six feet, with a solid metal door. A man standing in the center of the room could touch both walls. On each side of the room were concrete slabs, big enough for someone to lie down on, with iron stocks fastened to the ends. Jim found himself stretched out on one of those slabs, with his legs in the stocks. The stocks had been designed for a much smaller person. They were clamped down tight around Jim's ankles, cutting off any movement.

They left him there for weeks. The stocks rubbed his ankles raw, and the untreated sores became infected. They left him to urinate and defecate on himself, which also caused painful sores. Sometimes the guards came around with some soupy stuff, which they fed him without ever letting him out of the stocks. After a while he started to hallucinate.

There was a tiny drain in the floor for the periodic "cleaning" of the cell, which consisted of a guard splashing water on the floor. Most of Jim's hallucinations revolved around that hole in the floor. He would see a little wagon emerge from it, pulled by a tiny horse. A little man would climb out of the wagon and up onto Jim's concrete slab to give him a cigarette. Jim could just about taste that cigarette—but every time the cigarette was almost in his mouth, the hallucination would end abruptly.

In another recurring hallucination, he had escaped and was making his way through Laos. In the dream, he had to stay awake, or else they would put him back in the stocks. He would be hacking his way through the jungle in Laos, and just when he had almost made it to the other side, he'd wake up to find himself still in the stocks. The disappointment was unbearable.

The third recurring hallucination was the most pleasurable, and the worst. The metal doors throughout the prison were so loud that Jim could hear them opening and closing even in his sleep. Jim would dream that he was part of the ensemble of *Gunsmoke*. There he was, relaxing and drinking a beer in Miss Kitty's saloon, when suddenly he heard spurs coming his way. Now he was back in prison, and the outer door to the prison opened and Matt Dillon, the town marshal, came in. Matt Dillon ordered the guards, "Open these cells and let these prisoners out right now!" Then all the doors would come flying open, except they forgot about Jim. Jim would shout, "Wait! Wait! You missed my cell!" He was so agitated that he cried out in his sleep. Then the real guard would come in with his whisk broom and shove the handle into Jim's mouth to shut him up. That always woke him up fast.

The mental stress caused the most severe anguish, even worse than the physical torture and debasement. Sometimes Jim would hear other prisoners screaming, and that was worse than his own suffering. He couldn't stop himself from imagining what they were doing to the other guy. There was also the guilt. He had agreed to answer their questions, and he felt like a traitor. He should have been able to withstand more torture. He had been raised on John Wayne and World War II movies, he had seen people getting their fingernails pulled out and still not talking. He had been weak. He knew he must be the only soldier who had ever caved. These anguished ruminations hurt more than anything his captors could do to him.

He began to slip into hopelessness and despair. On the day of the crash, he'd made a split-second decision to eject from the plane rather than go down with it. Now, even if he wanted to end his life, he had no means. He couldn't even move in the tight iron stocks. Lying there on the concrete, drenched in his own urine and excrement, he was utterly, horribly trapped.

After weeks—Jim had no idea how long—they removed the stocks and moved him from the horrible cell. He still had a fever, but he was coherent. Both arms and both of his ankles were infected where the stocks had rubbed open his flesh, and he had raw, exposed sores all over his back side. His new room was bigger, and thankfully contained no stocks. The bed was a sawhorse with wooden planks across it and a thin rice mat. There was even a mosquito net, which was a God-send. After the last cell, this one felt like hog heaven. For several days he remained alone, and nobody came to bother him or ask him questions.

He must have been on the regular prison schedule now, because someone brought him food twice a day. It was diluted pumpkin soup, really just chunks of pumpkin floating in water, and sometimes rice. But Jim couldn't eat; everything came back up, and he was weak with dysentery. After he ate, or tried to, the guard came and opened the door to his cell, and Jim set his bowl outside. Other prisoners came and picked up the bowls and washed them. One time, Jim heard the soft whisper of an American voice through the door. The guard must have stepped away, and the prisoner on dish duty had taken a huge risk. His comforting words sang in Jim's ears: "Hey, new guy—we've all cooperated. Don't give up. We have all been through it. You are not alone. Do not give up."

His words hung in the air. Long after the American had walked away, the words echoed in the room and bounced off the walls of Jim's tiny concrete cell. Jim clung to them as if they were made of a tangible substance. Those few simple words of life, spoken by someone Jim would never meet, breathed hope and courage into Jim's spirit. He was not alone.

He sat up straighter on the wooden bed. He would not be defeated. He was a survivor. He was a fighter. He would not give up. He was not alone.

Chapter 8

Don't Let the Bed Bugs Bite

Hanoi, North Vietnam

Summer and Fall 1967

Sometime during the late summer of 1967, the North Vietnamese moved Jim from the Hanoi Hilton to a different prison. The guards came in the middle of the night, blindfolded and cuffed him, threw him in the back of a truck, and drove him to a camp called "The Zoo" by its inmates, tucked away in the southwest suburbs of Hanoi.

Once they had deposited him in his new cell, they removed the blindfold. He saw four bare walls, no window. A single, filthy light bulb hung from the ceiling. Rat droppings covered the concrete floor.

The room clearly accommodated more than one—there were three saw-horse "beds" with planks for mattresses, and one bucket in the corner for waste, already filled to the brim. The cell was hot and stuffy and stunk to high heaven.

Despite the revolting accommodations, Jim was glad about one thing. Bob Abbott, one of his flight buddies from combat crew training in Las Vegas, would be his new cellmate. Bob had been shot down five days before Jim. His other cellmate, Loren Torkelson, was another First Lieutenant, an F-4 Phantom pilot. Jim was thankful for these new cellmates. At least when he was able, he would have someone to talk to.

All three of the men were in bad shape. They suffered from diarrhea and dysentery, and, because they had not yet adjusted to their new diet or the unsanitary nature of their living conditions, they vomited constantly. The stench in the airless room was overwhelming, and with no ventilation it easily reached 140 degrees. The men had heat stroke, heat rash, bloody stool, and more output then their shared bucket could contain. Jim still had a violent fever and drifted in and out of consciousness as the infection from his arm wounds raged on. He had lost a frightening amount of weight, down to about 120 pounds on his 5'11" frame. His cellmates worried about losing him. They took turns feeding him soup and did all they could to keep him alive.[1]

The Zoo compound, previously used by the French as a film studio, had been converted temporarily in 1965 for use as a POW camp. Yards and yards of old film had been dumped in the old pool in the courtyard, and were now destroyed by rain water. The facility housed a hundred prisoners, with a separate annex holding about forty more. To convert the studio rooms into cells, the North Vietnamese had bricked up the windows and plastered over them, fixing a solid wood door to each room that only unlocked from the outside. The prisoners called it "The Zoo" because the gaps in the doors allowed the guards to peer in at the prisoners like animals in a zoo.

The guards gave each of the men their issue of clothing, consisting of a pair of black drawstring shorts, a black t-shirt, long pants, a long-sleeved shirt, and pajamas. It was one size fits all. The long attire had red and grey vertical stripes and a prison number. They generally wore the shorts every day because it was so hot, but when they had to go meet with a high-ranking North Vietnamese official for questioning (always a frightening ordeal that held the possibility of more torture), they had to wear their long attire and prison number. The regulation sandals were made from old tires—treaded soles with inner tube straps.

Once the turnkey guard burst in, pointed at Jim, and motioned for him to get dressed in the long pants and prison number. This was a bad sign. He tried to prepare himself for what might be awaiting him as he dressed and followed the guard down the hall and into another room of the compound. The interrogator was a small, mean man who called him "Chive-ly" and wanted Jim to describe the contents of a small plastic pill bottle containing tiny pellets. Jim recognized them as CBU pellets from the anti-personnel bombs the U.S. had dropped on Hanoi, but he pretended not to know what they were. After a tense exchange and a bit of grilling from the official, he was allowed to go.

TAPPING IN CODE

During World War II prisoners had communicated through Morse code. That didn't work in North Vietnam, because the prison walls were too thick to hear a "dash": two layers of brick with a plaster coating. So Jim and his fellow POWs devised their own method of tapping. Jim had learned about this first during his initial torture session. At one point when the guards had left the room, he had come to on the floor under a table. Someone had scratched a code matrix under the table, along with the instructions: "All prisoners learn this code." At the time Jim did not understand the significance of the markings, but now that he was surrounded by regular tapping, it didn't take him long to figure it out.

THE TAP CODE TABLE					
	1	2	3	4	5
1	A	B	C	D	E
2	F	G	H	I	J
3	L	M	N	O	P
4	Q	R	S	T	U
5	V	W	X	Y	Z

They took the alphabet and divided it into a 5x5 matrix, five rows and five columns. To identify a letter, the prisoner would tap the row first, and then the column. To tap a "c," they would tap once for row one, and then three times for column three. A "z" would be five taps for row five, then five more for column five. They left out the letter "k" since it could be replaced easily with "c."

When they wanted to communicate, they started by tapping, "Shave and a haircut." If it was clear and no guards were around, the response through the wall would be "two bits." If they received no answer, they knew to step away from the wall—there was a guard nearby. To be caught tapping was punishable by torture. While they communicated between cells, one man would tap while his cellmate lay near the door, peering through the gap between the bottom of the door and the concrete floor, watching for approaching feet. It got a little boring playing watch, so they would trade off. If they spotted a guard, they gave the danger signal: a loud thump, made by banging their elbow on the wall as they retreated from it. Everyone in the whole place backed away from their walls when they heard a thump. Generally, everyone knew a guard was approaching before he ever got close, because they could hear elbow thuds going on throughout the building.

Over time, the prisoners became adept at this method of communication and listening for various cues, and they learned the value of compression. For example, "When do you think we will go home?" became, "Wn Do U TK WE GO HOME?"

A more complicated message (with "x" as a sentence break) might read:

GM LGU Z 12 in PS Alrdy Hit F B10 x 5 now GETG THRTS F B10 X PB LTR FM HOME X LL FOX IS NEW XO x NEW NAME LCDR RENDER CRAYTON NO OTH INFO x PB N BP Q W SPOT SOS.

Translated, it meant:

Good morning. Larry Guarino says 12 men in Pig Sty have been tortured for biographies. Five men are now being threatened with torture if they do not write biographies. Phil Butler got a letter from home. Looks like Fox is the new executive officer of the camp. A new validated prisoner name is Lieutenant Commander Render Crayton. We have no other information on him. Phil Butler and Bob Peel had quizzes with Spot—same old shit.

To infuse some humor into their situation, the prisoners would try to make each other laugh. One night Major Sam Johnson sent the following communication to a prisoner in an adjoining cell, Commander James Stockdale: "GN GBU ST DLTBBB."

The message came as an evening signoff, made under duress, with both men on the lookout for spying guards. If caught, they would be punished. It took Stockdale a long time to decode, and when he finally did he laughed out loud at the risk Johnson had taken to tell him this: "Good night. God bless you. Sleep tight. Don't let the beg buds bite."[2]

THE PLANTATION

In the middle of one night, a guard came and moved Jim and his cellmates yet again. This time, it was to a prison they came to know as the Plantation, a relatively small camp in Northeast Hanoi, holding only about forty prisoners. The French had used it during the occupation as a small vehicle repair facility, so the cells were mini-garages converted into cellblocks. The three men were led into a fairly large room secluded from the rest of the camp. Instead of a single door, it had double doors that opened out and were secured from the outside with a padlock on a chain. "The Big House" where the officers lived and where they held interrogations stood in the center of the compound, and all the other buildings were clear across the courtyard. Because the three men were so far removed from the rest of the camp, they had no communication with anyone. They felt especially isolated. But they managed to find a way to look out and see the other prisoners by making a tiny hole in the door where there used to be a window. The guard never noticed. Looking out now and again to watch the other prisoners helped them to feel at least slightly connected to the outside world.

AIR RAIDS

KA-POW! Another explosion—Jim shot off his saw-horse bunk. That one was close. The summer of 1967 saw the most intense bombing in and around Hanoi. There were air raids almost every night, and at least twice a day. The bombs came startlingly close to the prison, making the whole building shake. The guards fired back with their AK-47s and anti-aircraft artillery. When the sirens went off, Jim, Loren, and Bob watched as the officials from the Big House scrambled into the big bomb shelter at the center of the camp. From the tiny hole in their door, Jim and his cellmates could tell the planes were getting close when the guards pulled out their AK-47s and helmets. As long as the guards remained standing with their weapons, they couldn't actually see any airplanes. Once they hunkered down into their individual bomb shelters, that meant they saw the planes. When the guards closed the lids to their shelters, the prisoners knew the U.S. planes were really close.

Raids served as a big morale booster for the prisoners. They knew their country had not forgotten them. Once they got used to the noise, the men actually enjoyed the night air raids because the guards turned off all the lights and went down to the shelters. The prisoners could talk to each other without being overheard and punished.

During one particularly violent raid, while the guards crouched in their shelters, a bomb exploded so close that Jim's ears rang, the floor of the cell bounced up and down, and the chain on the door blew off, flinging the door wide open. The three prisoners just sat there, stunned, and waited for the smoke to clear. In the spring of 1968, President Johnson stopped the bombing above the 20th parallel, and things quieted down. There were no more air raids.

SPECIAL TREATMENT

After the move to the Plantation, Jim, Bob, and Loren contracted hepatitis. Their skin and eyes turned yellow, and they were so sick and weak they could do nothing but lie on their beds. After the illness wore off, they began to realize that they were being treated better than the other prisoners in the camp. For one thing, they were allowed to bathe every day—a huge relief from the heat and stink of the cells, and from the heat rash they all contracted from sweating constantly. Bathing took place outdoors in a big concrete cistern, where each prisoner dumped a bucket of cold water over his body, while the guard stood by and made sure they didn't try to talk to anyone. From their peephole, Jim, Bob, and Loren noticed that the other prisoners only bathed once a week.

The three men also suspected they were getting better food that the others. Aside from the customary watered-down pumpkin soup with rice, and the occasional hunk of stale bread, the cellmates each received a banana. Uneasy, they wondered what garnered them these special privileges. They found out soon enough.

Chapter 9

Mind Games, Exploitation, and Propaganda

The Plantation

Fall 1967–Spring 1968

F or weeks after they arrived at the Plantation, Jim and his cellmates remained in isolation. No one even talked to them. They
were brought their food, taken out for their daily bath, and then
basically left to themselves. But as they recovered from hepatitis, the
guards started taking them in for "quizzes." This time, the appointments
were conducted by a high-ranking North Vietnamese government official
who spoke very good English. His questioning was much less violent
than the ones they had undergone at the Hanoi Hilton and the Zoo. Jim's
first appointment was mostly a lecture. The official sat him down and
gave him a history lesson on Vietnam, the Vietnamese-French, and their

war of independence from the French. Jim listened quietly and didn't say much.

TOURS AROUND TOWN

In the middle of one night, Jim woke with a start as the cell door opened. The cellmates jumped to their feet and bowed to the guards. They had learned the hard way that failure to bow meant swift and painful retribution. The guards handed them each a pile of civilian clothes and instructed them to dress. The sleepy men obeyed. Then the guards blindfolded them and led them outside, shoved them into a vehicle, and sped away.

The prisoners were dumbfounded and confused. At last the guards removed the blindfolds, and the three men found themselves in a bustling downtown area. People were shopping and eating, but mostly they stared at the Americans. The guards got them out of the Jeep and had them walk around, which was tense at first. Jim knew all too well what North Vietnamese townspeople were capable of. The guards, armed with AK-47s, kept the three men safe. With their civilian attire, Jim thought perhaps the idea was to make the townspeople think they were just important people being escorted around. An English-speaking guard relayed to them the reason for the tour. The North Vietnamese wanted the Americans to see for themselves that the bombing had not disrupted their lives. They had simply altered their schedules to spend time out and about at night. The country was as vibrant as it had ever been.

The next week the guards took them out during the day. The prisoners were driven to a part of Hanoi with significant bomb damage. Their tour guide told them: "This used to be a hospital, and you Americans bombed it. Do you see the blood on this doorpost? It is the blood of a doctor."

A week later they were driven to an orphanage and told the same thing.

Now they began to catch on to the game. The North Vietnamese officials were preparing them to accept an early release. Many POWs received this same offer, but Jim and his companions didn't know that yet, due to their isolation. To accept would have been in strict violation of the United States Military Code of Conduct, which states, "I will accept neither parole nor special favors from the enemy." To receive an early release, a POW had to "strike a deal" with the North Vietnamese, agreeing to speak out against his country and lie about the inhumane treatment received at the hands of his captors. If a released POW told the truth about the torture in the prison camps, the remaining inmates could be punished even more severely. To accept an early release violated both the POW's honor and the senior ranking officer's orders: they would leave only when all of the prisoners left, and they would leave in order of capture.

The guards soon dropped all pretense. They outright asked Jim and his cellmates, "How would you like to go home?"

Now they understood the special treatment, and they knew how it must look to the other prisoners. There was absolutely no way that

Jim, Loren, or Bob would even consider an early release, and they had long discussions in their cell about how to handle this absurd pressure. Should they risk punishment and just tell the North Vietnamese officials, "No way!" Or should they try to be more diplomatic? They decided to try an approach both diplomatic and firm. The next time they asked him if he wanted to go home, Jim replied, "Yes, sure, that would be nice. But I'm not going unless everyone goes."

This pressure went on for months during the fall and early winter of 1967. The North Vietnamese official would ask, "If we release you, what will you say about your treatment?" The men stood firm. They would absolutely tell the truth about the torture.

THE SHOWCASE

Part of the process of "wooing" Jim and his cellmates to accept an early release involved moving them into a newly constructed building on the Plantation premises. The cells were clean and had barred windows, fairly decent by North Vietnamese standards. They were especially grateful for the window. The only view was the back of the Big House, but at least it let in some fresh air, and the men could look out. They also had new neighbors, Joe Crecca and Doug Hegdahl, to communicate with. Joe, an Air Force pilot from Bloomfield, New Jersey, had been shot down near Hanoi by a surface-to-air missile in November 1966. Doug was a Navy enlisted man who had fallen off his ship and been captured the following April. Jim, Bob, and Loren soon learned that the North Vietnamese had been coaxing Crecca and Hegdahl to accept an early release as well.

This new building was known as the "Showcase," because the North Vietnamese used it as a ruse to convince delegates from other countries that all the prisoners were being housed fairly and decently. When a new international delegate or reporter arrived, he would be taken straight to the Showcase. The cells were kept clean, the corridors were scrubbed, and they planted gardens around it to make it look nice. They even forced the prisoners to pose for pictures there and then sent them back to the U.S. as an example of the general living conditions and treatment of the POWs. For one photograph they brought in a pool table and staged Jim and some of the others around it. After the picture was snapped, of course, they took the pool table away, and the prisoners never saw it again.

Visitors from eastern European countries also were invited to have a look in the windows, allowing the North Vietnamese to flaunt their humane treatment of their prisoners. The prisoners had been beaten to a pulp, tortured, and forced to lie for days and weeks in their own excrement before being moved to the Showcase. This exploitation only added insult to their injuries.

One night an American journalist visited them in the Showcase, accompanied by the guards. He even offered to take back any messages for their families. This special visit made it very clear to Jim and his cellmates that they were still being groomed for early release. They would have to be even more assertive about not wanting anything to do with it.

The North Vietnamese still had one more bizarre trip planned for Jim and his cellmates. They drove the three prisoners to a nice residential neighborhood in Hanoi, where French dignitaries had lived formerly. An East German film crew was using the neighborhood to make a movie, *Pilots in Pajamas*. There were other prisoners there as well. It was a complete set-up. The staged scenes showed them living in clean rooms, having access to showers, exercising, and eating healthy food. In fact, the whole film was a blatant propaganda tool, deliberately covering up the brutality with which the U.S. prisoners were treated, while making the North Vietnamese appear like the only true victims.

Apparently the North Vietnamese did not care for their performance in their ongoing "interviews" during this time. Jim, Loren, and Bob absolutely refused to lie and say the North Vietnamese were genial captors if they agreed to an early release. Eventually the officials tapered off their attempts to persuade them.

THE DUNGEON

By late 1967, when it became obvious that the men were not going to cooperate, Jim and his cellmates were moved out of the Showcase. Jim and Bob were relocated to another area of the Plantation called the Gun Shed—a cell so awful they took to calling it the Dungeon.

Loren Torkelson and Joe Crecca were put together in a building called the Warehouse. Doug Hegdahl remained in the Showcase.

The Dungeon was dark, wet, and disgusting. There was barely enough room for their two bunks and their shared waste bucket, and the door could only open halfway before it hit Bob's bunk when the guards came in. The men took turns walking back and forth in the narrow space between their bunks. It was atrociously dirty. Rats as big as small cats were especially attracted to the Dungeon because of dirty water that drained in and covered the concrete floor. Their droppings turned to mush beneath the prisoners' feet. Needless to say, the daily baths came to an abrupt end. The men were let out only one hour per week for a bath, or when it was their turn to empty the waste buckets. The cramped quarters, and the suffocating odor of the waste bucket, were just new forms of torture.

On top of all that, some of the other prisoners in the camp were pissed off at Jim and Bob for their previous special treatment. Resentment had been growing in the camp, but it was difficult to overcome since contact with the other prisoners was not allowed. Jim and Bob could only communicate through tapping, and it took some time to rebuild trust and solidarity with the rest of the camp.

The near-constant confinement in the tiny cell became virtually intolerable. Jim and Bob discussed everything under the sun, including cars, girls, friends, parents, siblings, their schooling, every book they had read, and every movie they had seen. At a certain point there simply was nothing more to talk about. Despite being good friends they started arguing. Every habit was magnified. One day when both men were lying in their bunks, Abbott kept tapping his fingers. It drove Jim to the brink of crazy.

Finally he screamed, "Dammit, Abbott, if you don't stop doing that, I'm going to beat the shit out of you!"

To which Bob replied, "Well if you don't stop whistlin', I'm going to beat the shit out of YOU!"

They made a pact: no more finger-tapping or whistling. After that they were able to coexist in the tiny space.

They remained stuck in the dungeon with the rats for about five months, bored out of their minds. In the early spring of 1968, desperate to see outside, Bob stood on Jim's shoulders to peer out the tiny closed window at the top of the cell. The window ledge broke, sending them toppling to the floor with a loud crash. The guards came running. They got in trouble, but it was worth it—the next day, the guards moved them to a bigger cell.[1]

DOUG HEGDAHL

Doug Hegdahl was already rather famous for his unique capture story. A Navy enlisted man, Doug had been accidentally knocked overboard from his ship. He floated in the Gulf of Tonkin for over five hours until he was picked up by a Vietnamese fisherman and turned over to the Viet Cong militia. They clubbed him almost to death before bringing him to the Hanoi Hilton, just one month before

Jim's capture. Only nineteen, Doug was incredibly smart, but he devised a plan to make himself appear stupid to the North Vietnamese. Whenever they brought him in for questioning, Doug pretended he could not read or write, prompting his captors to refer to him as, "the Incredibly Stupid One." His youthful appearance and country accent assisted in the ploy. Because the captors considered Hegdahl to be no threat, they gave him a lot more latitude and freedom than anyone else, even letting him do chores on the grounds. One of those "harmless" chores included putting dirt in the gas tanks of five trucks when he wasn't being watched. After Doug was through with them, each of the vehicles had to be towed away. The Vietnamese never caught on. He even managed to convince his captors that he couldn't see without glasses, so they didn't bother to blindfold him. On one drive into the city, he memorized the route from the prison into Hanoi.

He played dumb so well that the North Vietnamese decided to punish the senior officer prisoner, Commander Richard Stratton, by making Hegdahl his cellmate. Their plan backfired. The two quickly became friends, and they devised an arrangement for collecting information about the prisoners to take back to the States. This was the beginning of the unofficial "brain trust," a special group of prisoners dedicated to committing all the names of the POWs to memory so that there could be a full accounting.

As Hegdahl did his chores around the compound, he communicated with his fellow prisoners and collected information, unbeknownst to the North Vietnamese. He quietly memorized the names, capture dates, methods of capture, and Social Security numbers of more than 250 fellow POWs. With the help of Joe Crecca, his cellmate in the Showcase, he retained them all by putting them to the tune of "Old McDonald Had a Farm."

Over the years, the brain trust grew to include Jim Shively and Guy Gruters, among others. The men quietly committed all the names of the prisoners to memory by naming them off alphabetically using their fingers. The first list included their service and their name (with no regard for rank). The second list was name only. When another prisoner came in, they had to re-adjust the process to make room for the new name. The men in the brain trust counted off the names on their fingers as a daily exercise. By the end of the war, they had 352 names memorized.[2]

Hegdahl did not want to accept an early release, but Stratton ordered him to go. "Go ahead, blow the whistle," Stratton told him. "If it means more torture for me, at least I'll know why, and will feel it's worth the sacrifice." America needed to know how the prisoners were really being treated. Also, many of the prisoners' families, waiting helplessly back in the States for their men to return, had no way of knowing if their husbands and sons were dead or alive. Knowing that the information Hegdahl had committed to memory would not only provide invaluable information to the government, but would bring much comfort to the families as well, the other POWs agreed that Hegdahl's early release was warranted.

On August 5, 1969, Doug Hegdahl became the first authorized early release prisoner. In 1970, he was sent by the U.S. government to the Paris Peace Talks—where he confronted the North Vietnamese with his first-hand knowledge about the abuse of prisoners.[3]

At home in Spokane, Jim's family was frantic. His parents were glued to the television night after night, hoping for some coverage of the war. The video of Jim's capture happened to be one of the most widely circulated pieces of propaganda shown around the world. Jeanette Shively watched helplessly as her only son, blindfolded, handcuffed, and wounded badly, was paraded through the streets of Hanoi. She was not about to sit still while her son suffered that kind of violence. Back in the States, she was quickly becoming famous in her own right.

Chapter 10

"A Little Spark of Hope"

Spokane, Washington

June 1970

"Mothers should negotiate between nations. Mothers of fighting countries would agree: Stop this killing now. Stop it now."
—Yoshikani Taki

Jeanette paused at the platform, turned, and waved to the crowd below. She was grateful for the people who had turned out to see her off at Spokane International Airport. Many of them had contributed money to the adventure on which she was about to embark: a month-long tour around the world on behalf of the POWs in North Vietnam. She waved to Harold down below. Moments earlier, he had kissed her goodbye and told her he was proud of her.

Clara Jeanette Shively was made of tough stuff. Raised in the deep South in a strict, Southern Baptist home, she was not a woman to be put off or to accept defeat. For three years now, she had worked tirelessly on her son's behalf, and she was at the forefront of every possible movement to get him back. The lack of information the family had initially received concerning Jim was infuriating. They received word that he had been shot down and was being held in a North Vietnamese prison, and had seen him on television, but after that there was no news for several months, except the reports circulating about the inhumane treatment of the prisoners. The government told her she could send letters, but most of them were returned. She sent countless care packages, but she had no way of knowing if Jim ever received them.

Once the family received back an unopened card they had mailed to Jim, stamped with a message from the North Vietnamese: "Nobody to receive it—take it back." They refused to believe that Jim may have died in the prison camp. They knew it must be a deliberate, cruel ploy on the part of the North Vietnamese. In an interview, Jeanette announced, "We do not and will not accept what the return of the letter indicates until there is an inspection of the POW camps by a neutral international inspection team."

For months after that they lived day by day, moment by moment, hoping for a word from their son or some tidbit of information about him. "He needs more help than he ever has in his life," Mrs. Shively said, "but we are helpless ... "[1]

Finally, the Shivelys received a letter in Jim's handwriting. He was alive! But as Jeanette read it again and again, her concerns for Jim's condition were not alleviated. The tone and the phrasing were not her son's. Either the words had been dictated to him, or he was making things up so the North Vietnamese officials would actually mail the letter. He wrote things like:

Dear Mother and Father,

...the injuries I received when I ejected out of the machine have been treated very well and humanely. I have received good medical treatment. I have good quarters, and am allowed outside to get fresh air regularly. I have been very fairly treated. I eat well and I even have cigarettes to smoke, am given cookies and candy, and even lemon-water to drink. Give my love and greetings to my sister Phyllis and her husband Arlon.[2]

The letter made it sound like her son was away at summer camp. Clearly it was a ruse, and Jeanette was more fired up than ever to get her son back.

Disenchanted with what she perceived as government apathy, embodied in the president's promise that the American POWs would be returned "eventually," Jeanette turned up the heat. She was a special guest at a joint session of the Washington State legislature in Olympia when a memorial to Congress was passed urging the federal government to throw its full force behind every effort to gain more information about the POWs in North Vietnam.[3] Jeanette also joined the National League of Families of American Prisoners and Missing in Southeast Asia, a movement started by the wife of a captive, whose sole objective was to obtain the release of all prisoners.[4] She served as the area coordinator for the Eastern Washington chapter, affectionately referred to as "Rebel Leader" by the women who joined.[5] As a secretary in a local labor union for many years, Jeanette knew how to get things done and was known for her fearless, no-nonsense leadership. Harold joined in the meetings too, whenever he could.

In 1970, an opportunity arose for Jeanette and two other Spokane women in the League to embark on a month-long, worldwide tour to influence improvement in the North Vietnamese treatment of prisoners. They were to visit embassies in London, Paris, Stockholm, Prague, Bucharest, Belgrade, Rome, New Delhi, Laos, Thailand, and Tokyo. The journey was a huge undertaking, the result of thousands of hours of planning. It cost eight thousand dollars, financed mainly by donations from well-wishers in the Spokane community. Prior to the trip, the Spokane Chamber of Commerce wrote to every embassy requesting an appointment for Jeanette and her co-travelers, Faye Schierman and Marie Bossio, whose husbands were listed, respectively, as POW and MIA. Faye's husband, Wes, had been shot down in 1965. At the time of the trip, Marie had not had word from her husband in four years. Their mission: to draw attention to the number of prisoners being held captive in North Vietnam, to obtain any information possible on men listed POW or MIA, and to apply pressure on the neighboring countries to hold North Vietnam accountable for its inhumane treatment of prisoners.

The women elected Jeanette to be the spokesperson for the team because she was "very capable of handling any situation" and could "talk to any person in any country."[6] It turned out to be an emotionally exhausting whirlwind for three women just trying to help get their men back. In the course of their travels, they received a lecture from a Russian diplomat, had a door slammed in their faces, were rudely insulted, were called "insufficiently humble" in their request to obtain information, and were purposely driven to a wrong location. They were also blessed, prayed for, listened to intently, and had a young, scared, female interpreter fall apart on their shoulders. In Laos, the official in charge refused to meet with them. Instead they were taken to a low-level embassy official who lectured them and repeatedly assured them that the captured prisoners were being humanely treated. While in Rome, however, they were graciously received and had a long interview with an assistant to the pope, who blessed their trip and prayed for their men.

It was up one day and down the next, but they remained steadfast and determined in their mission. By the time they returned to Spokane, they were hopeful that they had raised worldwide awareness and concern for the prisoners. As soon as they landed, the women held a press conference. Jeanette reported that many leaders worldwide were willing to work for the POWs privately, especially after the women's visit brought the problem so clearly to their attention. "We feel the effort we made will be continued through the governments we visited and through the Red Cross. As long as there is a little spark of hope, families will be encouraged to blow on that spark."[7]

Chapter 11

Hanoi Hannah, Gyro Gearloose, and Ladies' Underwear

The Plantation

1968–1970

J im grabbed his regulation washcloth, really just a dirty scrap of thin fabric, and stood on his "bed" to reach the filthy light bulb. He wrapped the piece of cloth around it until it got scorching hot, and then held it to his left ear. He was in tremendous pain. His nasty ear infection had been going on for about two years now, exacerbated by the dirty water he now had to bathe in. The light bulb trick had stopped helping months ago, and his requests for medical attention were continually ignored. The ear was now constantly issuing pus, and Jim could no longer hear out of it. He had to pull the lobe down to try to open the passage way to the ear drum.

Following the broken window ledge, Bob and Jim had been moved into a bigger, four-man cell with Loren Torkelson and Joe Crecca. The men were concerned about Jim. In the Dungeon, Bob had helped Jim by pushing on the back of his ear to relieve the pressure and allow the pus to discharge. Jim never complained and tried not to show discomfort. Now, the ear was continually draining itself, and the pain was so great that he could barely sleep or eat.

His cellmates lobbied the guards on Jim's behalf. Finally, they sent in a medic, a white-coated man armed with a very large, very dull needle. Joe Crecca called it "the caulking gun." It dug way into Jim's thigh before it finally broke skin. Jim was not at all convinced the man was a real doctor, but at this point he would take whatever help he could get. The medic gave him a painful shot of what Jim hoped was penicillin, which provided no relief. On the fourth day Joe Crecca suggested the medic squirt the medicine directly in Jim's ear and see if that would help. Not understanding, the medic aimed the needle directly at Jim's ear. The sight of that huge, blunt instrument of pain coming right for his head was too much. Jim, already dizzy from fever, clutched the corner of the bed to keep from passing out. He heard Joe scream, "No!" Startled, the medic stopped. Joe made a squirting sound and mimicked a stream into his ear. This time, the medic understood, and a greatly relieved Jim felt the medicine slip directly into his red-hot ear canal. This unorthodox delivery method went on for a few more days until, at last, the ear ache went away. Later, Jim's doctors back in the States told him an exterior application of penicillin could not have done any good. Just the same, the infection was gone and it never came back.

Earlier in their imprisonment, the prisoners sometimes went three to four weeks without a bath, despite sweating constantly in the extreme heat. Because he was always sweaty and dirty, Jim had developed an infection beneath his skin which caused huge, painful boils on his back and legs. These would grow to enormous size before they burst and pop, and they were a source of constant aggravation. Other prisoners suffered boils too, but none seemed to be as extreme as Jim's. When he received medical attention years later, he learned it was because he had "extra small" pores.

Across the board, medical care was hard to come by. Some of the men in the Plantation grew severely asthmatic and nearly died before they were administered adrenaline. Before being in North Vietnam, none of them had suffered from asthma. Later they learned that there was a particular tree growing nearby that caused an allergic reaction.

Once a pink eye epidemic swept through the camp. Virtually no one escaped, not even the guards. Everyone's eyes swelled shut, and the entire camp was essentially blind for days.

A STABILIZING INFLUENCE

Jim's three cellmates looked up to him. Loren, as the highest ranking officer, was considered the official leader, but Jim, quiet, calm, and wise for his years, was a natural leader. When he spoke, his words carried weight. He was well educated and knowledgeable about political science and world events, but more than that, he didn't have a big ego or high ambitions. He was even-keeled and had a rare gift for seeing the humor in everything. He refused to let his circumstances dictate his emotions.

While the other men occasionally fought, Jim provided a "calm, stabilizing influence," in the words of his cellmate Joe Crecca.[1] One time Crecca and Abbott got into a yelling match that nearly came to blows. Jim stepped calmly in between them and broke it up, doing his best to make the situation humorous until they both cooled off.

Jim made a concentrated effort not to waste time feeling sorry for himself. At first he had entertained self-pity, wondering, "Why did this happen to me? I'm a nice guy." For five or six months he wished he hadn't ejected from his plane. But eventually he decided to stop brooding. It didn't do any good, and he could either get busy living, or get busy dying. He determined to live by taking it one day at a time and by not looking too far into the future.

According to Crecca, most prisoners would only allow themselves to project six months into the future. If they weren't home by then, they'd project another six months. When the air raids were most intense, some POWs would predict that the air raids were the "last big push of the war." For some reason, Jim was able to be more realistic. Once Crecca asked him if he thought they would get out soon.

Jim Shively as a toddler. *Courtesy of Nancy Shively*

F-105 Thunderchief taking off. *Courtesy of Wikimedia Commons*

"The Elite 8," F-105 combat training at Nellis AFB, 1966. Front: Bob Abbott, Paul Sheehy, Bob Lodge, Gary Smith. Back: Jim Shively, Gary Mathews, Gordon Jenkins, Bob Weskamp. *Courtesy of Gordon Jenkins*

Hoa Lo Prison.
Courtesy of U.S. Air Force

First Lieutenant James R. Shively.
Courtesy of the author

The ropes torture.
Drawings by Mike
McGrath. *Reprinted, by
permission, from John M.
McGrath, Prisoner of War: Six
Years in Hanoi (Annapolis, Md:
Naval Institute Press, ©1975)*

Jim Shively as a prisoner of the North Vietnamese. *Courtesy of the Shively family*

Loren, Joe, Bob, and Jim prepare a very unhappy Thanksgiving dinner at The Plantation, 1968. *Courtesy of Joe Crecca*

Kissinger's Twenty arrive at Hanoi's Gia Lam Airport on the day of their release, February 18, 1973. *Courtesy of Joe Crecca*

POW camps around Hanoi. *Courtesy of Mike McGrath*

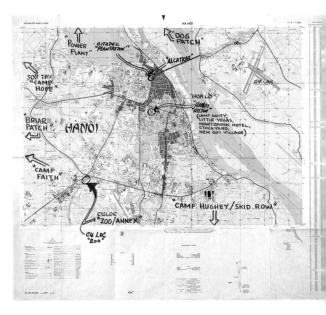

Jim walking as a free man for the first time in nearly six years, with his welcoming officer at Gia Lam Airport, Hanoi, February 18, 1973. *Courtesy of the author*

Jim Shively reunited with his parents at Travis Air Force Base. *Courtesy of Chris Gilliland*

One of the many POW bracelets that have been sent to the Shively family since Jim's return. *Courtesy of the author*

Jim, Nancy, and their four girls in 1982. *Courtesy of Nancy Shively*

In a special ceremony in 1992, Speaker of the House Tom Foley presented Jim with the medals that were destroyed in the house fire: two Purple Hearts, two Silver Stars, one Bronze Star, one Distinguished Flying Cross, four Air Medals, and one Legion of Merit. *Courtesy of the author*

Jim and Nancy on Halloween, circa 2000. *Courtesy of the author*

Jim and Nancy Shively, Christmas Day, 1994. *Courtesy of the author*

Jim and his girls: Nikki, Amy, Jane, and Laura at his retirement party in 2004.
Courtesy of the author

"Any day you can turn the handle on the door and walk out of the room…is a good day." —Captain James Richard Shively, 1942–2006.
Courtesy of the author

Jim replied, without hesitation, "No. It will be another five years." Crecca later said Jim had an uncanny "knowing" about when the war would end, and as it turned out, he was exactly right.[2]

The men who pinned their hopes on an end date suffered more emotional ups and downs. Small improvements in living conditions made them elated, thinking they'd be going home soon, which only led to bigger letdowns and more depression when things didn't go as they hoped. In Crecca's words, Jim was so even-tempered that you would never know if he was depressed or not. A smile would come to his face very easily if something funny happened. Jim's choice to live, laugh, and take it one day at a time became a source of strength for other prisoners who were struggling.

PRISON LIFE

Prisoners at the Plantation were luckier than many other American POWs—they got two meals every day. The diet varied little, consisting almost entirely of soup and rice, or soup and stale bread, served with what the prisoners jokingly referred to as their "side dish." The soup was hot water with something floating in it, usually chunks of pumpkin, sometimes a mystery green vegetable that had a nasty petroleum taste. The prisoners called the green vegetable "kerosene greens." The side dish was more of whatever vegetable had been tossed into the soup that day. Often the men discovered rodent parts and insects in their food. A cellmate of Jim's once let out a yell after biting into a piece of bread. His bread was full of big, fat worms, and he had bitten into one—and it bit him back.

The prisoners were allowed three "luxuries" a day, which came in the form of cigarettes. For the rest of his life, Jim attributed his smoking addiction to the fact that cigarettes had been his only pleasure for six years. Each morning, the guard would open the Judas window, a pane of glass that let the prison guards see into the cell without being seen by the prisoners, and handed in three cigarettes per person. Then he would hold out a punk stick, and one of the prisoners would have to get a light and pass it around. The guards came around with the punk stick first thing in the morning, after the first meal, and again after dinner. They made sure the prisoners didn't enjoy their small luxury too much, barely giving them time to light up before they took the punk stick away. If you missed it, the men in your cell were out of luck.

The prisoners smoked their cigarettes down as low as they could, and then saved any remaining tobacco. When they had enough accumulated they would roll another one. They did this using the camp toilet paper, which was another extravagance they used as sparingly as possible. The toilet paper came to them in rations, in big 8x8 sheets, very coarse and brown, and so un-refined that there were chunks of wood in it. They had to be extremely judicious in their use, tearing it off in small increments. Whatever they managed to spare, they used for hand-rolled cigarettes.

The toilet paper had several other uses as well. Unbeknownst to the guards, the prisoners devised a way to pass notes to each other by writing on the hearty toilet paper with their toothpaste tubes. The toothpaste, which came once every three months, was in a lead tube, with an end so pointy they could write with it. The latrine facility was simply a bucket with a little metal band holding the lid together. Naturally, it had to be emptied every day. Every morning a guard would open the door, and the men would set their buckets out. One cell was assigned to take them to the outhouse to dump and rinse them, and bring them back. The men tucked notes to each other inside the metal bands. One crew would read the note, tuck it back in the band, and deliver it to the next building. The notes had to be very small, but it was enough to inform each other of names of new people in the camp and other valuable information. The prisoners had covert signals for acknowledging receipt of information, too. If a new message had been received and read, the prisoner exiting the outhouse would scratch himself on the way out.

They also passed information from building to building through their laundry. On bath day they washed out their clothes and hung them up on the line to dry. Of course, everyone's clothes looked the same and were the same size. Notes fit nicely in the drawstring waistband of the pants, so they would purposely pick up the wrong clothes.

The men fell in to the basic camp routine. In the morning they emptied waste buckets and brought in the daily quota of cigarettes. Each individual cell also had a routine in place. Between the first morning cigarette and breakfast, room-to-room communication (in the form of tapping) took up a good part of the morning. It was a group effort because one person had to lie on the floor to watch for the guard, and then they would switch places. Cells with a neighboring cell on either side had to tap on both walls. They also tried to get some exercise in the mornings, pacing up and down the tiny room. This morning schedule was interrupted once or twice a week by a cold bath—a welcome respite from the heat and the cramped cell.

After the first meal and their second cigarette, it was siesta time. Sleep provided a welcome escape from reality. After their nap they went back to tapping before the second meal and the last cigarette. Tapping stopped as it got dark, since it was harder to see the guards coming. In the evenings the cellmates chatted with each other. To pass the time they conducted literary and film reviews, discussing in detail every book they had ever read, and every movie they had ever seen. They knew everything there was to know about one another's former lives.

From 8:30 until 9, they had to listen to "Hanoi Hannah," an English-speaking broadcast that was beamed to the GIs in South Vietnam each day. Every one of the cells had a speaker, and the prisoners had no control over the volume or the on-off switch. The show was pure propaganda. According to Hannah, the Viet Cong were winning the war and enjoyed "great victories" every day. Despite the North Vietnamese disinformation, the POWs could decipher some of what was happening in the world, and the ebb and flow of the war. At the end of every program, Hannah would list the GIs killed in battle the day before. She also reported on the anti-war movement and the 1968 election in the States. One rather peculiar report relayed to its listeners how much wiser and more technologically advanced the Russians were than the Americans, because they had put a remote control device on the moon, which did not endanger any astronauts. From this broadcast, the prisoners gleaned that America had landed a man on the moon.

At about 9:00 every night, the guards rang a bell sending the prisoners to bed. Jim's bed at the Plantation consisted of two saw-horses with wooden planks nailed together on top, with a thin mat woven out of rice straw to lie on. He rolled up his clothes for a pillow. There were no blankets, and in winter the prisoners froze, the cold going way past shivering and into a bone-chilling ache. It was quite a ritual every night getting tucked in under the mosquito net, making sure there were no mosquitoes trapped under the net with him. They had to sleep with the light on, except during night air raids when the guards turned them off.

The families of the prisoners wrote constantly, but most correspondence was hijacked by the North Vietnamese. When the prisoners actually received their mail, it was usually connected with propaganda. For example, one time at Christmas Jim was invited to the Big House for a quiz, and they gave him a letter from home. Then they took his picture while he read it, to send back to the States to show how well they treated the prisoners. The letters were always highly censored, with whole phrases blacked out. Jim enjoyed the sporadic messages from home, although it was not quite the big deal for him that it was for the men who were married with families. One time, his cellmate got a letter with a picture of his new baby girl, who had been born after his capture. That was an exceedingly rare, very special occasion.

The prisoners received the care packages their families sent to them even more rarely. Boxes could weigh just a little over two pounds, and the guards confiscated all the fun stuff, like playing cards, pencils, paper, and books, before the parcel ever made its way to the intended recipient. By the time they got it, usually only soap and underwear were left. Once Jim received a package from home of what had been chocolate and clothes. But the clothes were shredded to rags and the chocolate had been pounded into dust.

The prisoners were sometimes allowed to send letters home, but only because of anti-war delegations who visited from eastern Europe. The North Vietnamese would give the POWs special forms to write on, and then send the forms back with the delegates as a way to show the world how well they were treating the American prisoners. Initially, only known captives were allowed to write, and the letters were heavily censored by the North Vietnamese. The men could only write about their family and their health—and they had to say that their health was good.

GYRO GEARLOOSE

The guards were mean, and they all carried AK-47s with bayonets. Often they prodded the prisoners in the back with their weapons, to hurry them along. The prisoners had nicknames for every guard. One they called "Gyro Gearloose" after the Walt Disney character with crossed eyes and a shock of messy hair. One time, Gyro Gearloose was taking Loren Torkelson to the Big House for a quiz, and he shoved him with the AK-47 a little too hard. Without thinking, Torkelson spun around and grabbed the gun out of his hands. With a shock of terror, he realized what he had done. The guards stationed on the towers could shoot him at any second. He was close to the Big House, so he threw the weapon inside an open door and listened as it clattered loudly all the way down the long hallway and out an open door on the other side. He marched into the meeting room and just sat there, scared out of his wits, sure he would be punished with extreme torture. To his surprise, the North Vietnamese officials came in, conducted an uncommonly short interview, and left without a word about Torkelson's insurgence. Instead, the prisoners never saw Gyro Gearloose again.

PRISON ANTICS

The prisoners at the Plantation tried to keep a sense of humor, mostly at the expense of the North Vietnamese guards, or the "V." As the years went by, in order to keep themselves entertained, the prisoners messed with the officials as much as they could get away with it. Sometimes to distract them during interviews, the prisoners would stare intently at the wall behind them, pass gas, sneeze profanities, or say the wrong words on purpose. For a while, the prisoners raised their middle fingers for staged photographs, which the V mistook for the equivalent of a "thumbs-up." This was one way for them to let the U.S. know the "cheerful" pictures were bogus. They got away with this for a few years before the V caught on.

Overall, the V were not very clever. Sometime in 1968, in a meager attempt to improve the conditions of the camp, the North Vietnamese built three bathhouses for the prisoners. They were built side by side, each containing a solitary cistern, with one connecting drain. Communication between the prisoners at bath time was absolutely forbidden, punishable by torture, but the prisoners could hear each other just by whispering through the shared drain system. It took a while for the V to catch on, but once they figured it out, they kept a guard posted close by and left the middle room vacant.

Unlike some of the other camps, there was no forced labor at the Plantation, but the prisoners did have some chores, like washing dishes after meals or fertilizing the camp's vegetable garden by scooping out waste from the outhouse and using a stick to spread it around the plants. Another messy job was making coal balls, termed CBUs (coal ball units) by the men. Coal got delivered to the camp as dust. The prisoners would make baseball-sized briquettes by mixing the dust with special mud. They had to use their feet to do the mixing and their hands to form the coal balls. It took weeks to get the coal bits out from under their fingernails, toenails, and the cracks of the skin. The whole process took several hours, and many of the prisoners hated the task, but Jim didn't really mind. It provided a welcome break from the cell. Also, the regular turnkey guards would leave them in the care of the wall patrol guards, who weren't nearly as mean. They spoke no English, but the prisoners would strike up conversations with them using sign language. Once they became friendly, the prisoners could sometimes wheedle an extra cigarette out of them. One time Jim even stole some matches while his cellmate distracted the wall patrol guard with meaningless gestures.

Life fell into a kind of routine, but the prisoners were always on edge, never knowing when a guard might burst into their cell at a random time. These non-routine visits never boded well for them, and they could happen at any time of the day or night. The POWs lived in constant dread of an unexpected visit and a trip to the Big House, which always had the potential to end in torture. The least dangerous of these meetings were what the V called "attitude checks." The V were continually checking on the prisoners' attitudes about the war, on the lookout for POWs who would cooperate with them and renounce their own country.

Sometimes the V conducted these meetings just to bone up on their English, so the prisoners would deliberately try to teach them the wrong words. Jim had one funny attitude check the second Christmas he was there. He received a package from home, and the guards had gone through it, removing cigarettes and other things they wanted, but leaving some of it intact. Later, Jim got called down to the Big House. The interrogator wanted to know why he had received ladies' underwear. Apparently, in North Vietnam only women's underwear had an opening in front, never men's. Jim tried, but he could not convince them that the reverse was true in the States.

The prisoners usually got a special meal at Christmas, for propaganda purposes. It was chicken or turkey, and the North Vietnamese would kill the birds by pinning their wings back and slitting their throats. One year, there was a Japanese film crew there, so the V decided to have the prisoners kill the turkey. The prisoners insisted on doing it their way. They asked for a hatchet, held the twenty-pound bird down, chopped off its head, and then let it loose. Chaos ensued. It flopped and flapped everywhere, squirting blood all over the men and the Japanese film crew. The prisoners thought it was a riot, but the camp commander was livid. He chased the bird all over the grounds, shouting in Vietnamese and cussing at the men. Finally, the guards sent them all back to their cells covered in turkey blood. They all agreed it was worth it just to see the looks on the V's faces—and the film crew.

Another time, the V ordered the prisoners to write about Tet, the Vietnamese New Year. Their essays would be sent back home, to show how much "fun" the prisoners were having. That year happened to be the "Year of the Cock." You can imagine some of the witticisms the prisoners slipped into their essays. The V even read some of them aloud over the intercom system before they mailed them. The entire camp was howling, but the guards never got the joke.

It went on this way for a while for Jim and the other inmates at the Plantation. They did their best to hold up under the boredom, the cramped conditions, hoping not to be picked out by the guards for "punishment," reveling in the occasional comic relief.

But things were about to change drastically—for the worse.

Chapter 12

Escape and Repercussions: New Levels of Hell

Hanoi, North Vietnam

May 1969

"We are...pressed, but not crushed...persecuted, but not abandoned, struck down, but not destroyed."

—Saint Paul

Members of the United States Armed Forces are bound by the U.S. Military Code of Conduct, which states that a prisoner of war "will make every effort to escape and aid others to escape."[1] On May 10, 1969, Captain John Dramesi and Lieutenant Colonel Edwin Atterberry, prisoners held in the Zoo, slipped through the roof of their cell and managed to escape the prison compound. They were able to travel three miles before they were recaptured the next day. Theirs was not the first escape in North Vietnam. There had been a few other attempts, all of which ended badly.

Ernie Brace, the longest-held civilian prisoner in North Vietnam, was a civilian pilot employed by a cargo company. He had been delivering supplies and passengers to Laos when his aircraft was suddenly riddled with enemy fire. Immediately captured by the North Vietnamese Army, Ernie spent a few of his seven years as a prisoner in a bamboo cage in the jungle, his feet in stocks and an iron collar around his neck. He managed to escape three times, but was recaptured every time. After his third attempted escape they buried him in the ground up to his neck. He was beaten, starved, and humiliated, eventually becoming paralyzed from his imprisonment in a four-foot high cage that decreased to two feet at one end.[2]

It was courageous to attempt escape, but in North Vietnam the POWs had nowhere to run once they got out of the prison camp. White Americans simply did not blend in. Dramesi and Atterberry made it as far as the river, but once daylight came, they had nowhere to hide. The river was a very populated place during the day, and although they had used iodine to darken their skin, a Vietnamese fisherman found them hiding in the reeds.

The repercussions of the Dramesi/Atterberry escape attempt proved brutal for everyone. Every prisoner at the Zoo was tortured severely. Some guards were utterly sadistic, seeming to get a thrill out of the beatings. Captain Dramesi was forced to lie face down on a table, and while one guard held his head down, the others beat him with a four-foot length of rubber from an old tire. They beat him for days on end, in ninety-minute sessions. Afterwards he was placed on a near-starvation diet and subjected to the ropes torture for thirty-eight days. Ed Atterberry was last seen by another prisoner being taken from his cell in a bloody mess. He died under torture on May 18. The V told his fellow POWs he died of an "unusual disease."[3]

The North Vietnamese did not confine retribution to the Zoo. The entire POW population in North Vietnam was systematically punished for the attempted escape. Some men, thought to be involved in the planning of the escape, were taken out of their cells and tortured severely every day for weeks. The food got worse, and the torture was atrocious. Methods varied from one camp to another. Some prisoners were burned with cigarettes, some had bamboo slivers pushed into their fingers and their thumbnails peeled back, and some underwent electrical shock torture, administered with two bare wires plugged into a wall outlet.[4]

Prisoners were forced to undergo interrogations on their knees for hours or even days, until their knees became flattened, red, and swollen. One prisoner named Mike McGrath, a lieutenant commander in the U.S. Navy, spent thirty hours on his knees as punishment for peeking out of the vent in his cell. He was then taken to the sidewalk outside and beaten with a section of rubber tire.[5] Rope binding was another popular form of torture, resulting in burns that became infected and left permanent, ugly scars. Some men were hung upside down from rafters and then beaten unconscious and left there. The guards would remove their shoes and sneak back into the room in the middle of the night to cut the prisoner down while he slept. If he screamed he got a dirty rag shoved into his mouth and pushed down his throat with an iron bar. If a prisoner resisted, the guard would break his teeth with the iron bar.[6]

The V wanted to inflict not just pain, but humiliation and degradation upon their captives. Jim was among the prisoners who were taken to an area on a hillside where three-foot holes were dug into the ground, covered by black doors. The prisoners called these "black boxes." They were forced inside, where they sat in six inches of water in the pitch dark, with their hands bound behind their backs so they could not defend themselves against the swarms of mosquitos. Their hands were so tightly bound that the metal cut through the skin to the bone. They were left in the boxes for days at a time and contracted dysentery, and were forced to relieve themselves in their clothes. The stench was so overwhelming that even the guards would not come near.[7]

After the Dramesi/Atterberry escape attempt, the captured U.S. senior ranking officers modified the code of conduct. Now the POWs were ordered not to attempt escape unless they had a possibility of getting out of the country, or could count on receiving some kind of underground assistance from outside the camp. The escape attempts ceased after that, but the POWs remained under the constant threat of torture.

Jim and his cellmates survived, but many others didn't. The excessive brutality killed at least two prisoners and drove others to the brink of insanity.[8] The horrific reports clouded all of the camps in darkness and despair. Whatever hope the POWs had been clinging to had been viciously snuffed out. They grew daily more convinced that they would be dead before they would be free.

Chapter 13

Camp Faith

North Vietnam

September 1969–January 1972

J im and his cellmates looked at each other pointedly. It was September 1969, and Hanoi Hannah had just announced over the radio broadcast that Ho Chi Minh, president of North Vietnam, was dead. The men held their breath. What would this mean for them? Would the war end? Would treatment get better, or worse? Even the guards were noticeably on edge, much more than normal.

Thankfully, after Ho Chi Minh's death treatment in the camps generally improved, and the torture interrogations eventually came to a halt. In some camps, the men stopped bowing. They were allowed to bathe more regularly. They even received thin blankets to use at night. Most notably, they were moved to bigger rooms, each housing six or seven men, which gave them more people to interact with each day. It was a welcome change.

At the time, the prisoners could not know what accounted for the improvements. Later they found out that pressure had been put on the North Vietnamese by other governments who were now aware of the severe mistreatment of the prisoners. In early 1969 the North Vietnamese had received a confrontational visit from U.S. Secretary of Defense Melvin Laird, who was armed with pictures of severely beaten and starved prisoners, taken by foreign news services.

Laird told the North Vietnamese: "The Geneva Convention says that you shall release all sick and wounded prisoners. These men are sick and wounded. Why aren't they released?"[1]

In response, on August 5, 1969, three American POWs were released, including Doug Hegdahl, who spoke candidly about the starvation and torture. Hegdahl had lost seventy-five pounds. Navy Lieutenant Robert Frishman had been returned to the United States having lost an elbow and sixty-five pounds. Also released was Air Force Captain Wes Rumble, who was in a body cast because of a broken back. After their press conferences, headlines about the abuse appeared all over the world. The North Vietnamese were found to be clearly in contempt of the Geneva Convention, which led to pressure from other governments.

Another considerable improvement for Jim occurred in July 1970, with the opening of a new prison camp. There were fourteen camps in and around Hanoi, but now the North Vietnamese closed some of the smaller camps, and started consolidating the men into larger ones.[2] The majority, 220 men, were brought to the new Dan Hoi prison, located nine miles west of Hanoi.[3] It was a series of walled compounds, with each building being made up of two large rooms. Each room accommodated sixteen to twenty men, with open windows to provide much-needed ventilation. For the first time, the men were allowed to associate in large numbers.

The guards now let the men out into the center of the compound, one room at a time, for an hour or two each day. During that time they could go to the well and bathe, or they could just mingle. The guards also left the windows open in the other rooms during this time, so the men who were out could chat with the men inside. The food improved a little bit, too, prompting some to believe that they were being fattened up for release.

They weren't. Release was still several years away, but these improvements in socialization and physical exercise were instrumental in reviving everyone's disposition. The conditions were so improved at this camp that the men nicknamed it "Camp Faith." Hope was in the air again.

SON TAY PRISON RAID

Then, on November 20, 1970, all hell broke loose at Camp Faith. Since the U.S. bombings had stopped in 1968, the prisoners were accustomed to hearing only the occasional unmanned drone. Now, without warning, airplanes and anti-aircraft warfare filled the air above them, lighting up the sky with explosion after explosion. They didn't know it at the time, but it was the American military performing a rescue attempt at Son Tay Prison, about fifteen miles from Camp Faith. In an audacious effort to rescue the sixty-five prisoners they believed were housed there, the American military intentionally landed a helicopter in the middle of Son Tay and proceeded to seize control. Unfortunately, the Son Tay prisoners had been moved to another camp. The U.S. pulled off the mission with no loss of American life, and only one wounded. Between one hundred and two hundred North Vietnamese soldiers were killed in the raid.

Despite being a botched rescue attempt, the mission was considered a success because it rattled the North Vietnamese government significantly, putting a world-wide spotlight on the American POWs and their treatment. That modified how the North Vietnamese housed and interacted with the prisoners. Moreover, the mission sent a clear message to the Russian and Chinese governments who were assisting the North Vietnamese: America would go to any lengths to rescue her men.

The raid boosted the spirits of the prisoners. They knew their government had not forgotten or abandoned them.[4]

The very next day after the raid, high-ranking North Vietnamese officials came and toured Camp Faith. Apparently they decided it was not secure enough, because the prisoners were moved the following day back to the Hanoi Hilton. Arriving again at the Hilton, they found all the POWs in North Vietnam had been relocated there. Although it made for cramped quarters, the 339 men were more than happy to be consolidated. They had to be put in much larger groups now, accommodating forty to sixty prisoners. The lodgings were long, warehouse-style buildings with concrete floors and rows of windows near the roof. The best part was that every room included an actual walled-off bathroom—really just a hole in the floor, but with a closed door for privacy.

They could still be punished for it, but communication between rooms was now relatively easy. They all lived on the same side of the camp, with open windows between each of the cells, so the prisoners simply stood on their concrete bunks and looked into their neighbors' cells to signal and communicate covertly, while their cellmates kept a lookout for guards.

MIKE BURNS

Undergoing such severe sufferings together for years on end, the POWs forged lifelong friendships. Mike Burns became one such friend for Jim. An Air Force pilot from Fort Wayne, Indiana, Mike had been flying an F-4 when it was shot down over the North Vietnam pan-handle. He was captured, beaten, and thrown in the back of a truck, where he remained bound for thirty-five days as it transported him to Hanoi. Mike had heard of Jim Shively through the POW grapevine.

He knew Jim was an F-105 pilot who had been a top Air Force Academy graduate, and that Jim was part of the brain trust. He considered Jim an "old-timer" and a "tough guy" because he was known as one of the strongest resistors to have undergone the earliest interrogation torture sessions.

Mike was impressed by Jim. He would later recall:

> I remember when I first met Jim, I saw the terrible large boils on his back and I saw the gouges out of both ankles caused by the leg irons put down on him hard during his torture sessions. But even when he was telling me how his ankles were mangled, he did it with that easy laugh of his.

Jim earned respect, not because he vied for it, but because he treated everyone patiently and with esteem, including the loudest and most disagreeable among them. One evening, one of the men got angry because some other guys were talking. The perturbed prisoner announced that all talking must stop *now*, because he wanted silence. The situation could easily have become a fight, and the other men instinctively looked to Jim. Jim's quiet smile said, "Let it go." They did.

Since Mike hadn't been shot down until 1968, he had seen *The Graduate*, starring Dustin Hoffman and Anne Bancroft. Some of the prisoners in the cell next to them had heard about the movie, which had been a big hit in the States, and they wanted a scene-by-scene review. Jim was nominated to do the reenactment, which was going to be a risky endeavor. Despite the recent improvements, one thing hadn't changed, and that was the threat of beatings if the prisoners were caught talking. The reenactment would have to be through the open window, at night, quietly, so the guards wouldn't hear. In the safety of their cell, Mike recounted the entire movie to Jim from beginning to end, changing the tone of his voice for the different characters, and adding sound effects for the little Alfa Romeo convertible, going through all the gears as it raced down the highway. Jim listened intently, with no questions or interruptions. When Mike was done, he asked Jim if he had any questions or wanted Mike to do a scene over. "Nope, I got it," was Jim's reply. Mike was amazed the next night when Jim retold the movie, every detail intact, complete with sound effects, to the prisoners next door, without having reviewed it and without any notes. It was a huge hit.

HANOI UNIVERSITY

The prisoners spent all but one or two hours each day penned up in their cells, growing increasingly frustrated by the feeling that their lives were being wasted. They had nothing to occupy their time, like playing cards or books, because the guards worried about secret messages coming in. So the men set up a secret school system. They figured out each one's area of expertise and appointed a Dean responsible for scheduling courses and designating room space. They called it "Hanoi University."

During the day they held classes. Language classes were especially popular. Two of the men were native Spanish speakers, and their classes were in high demand. Some men spoke fluent French, others German.

Jim taught Russian, which he had learned at the Air Force Academy, as well as courses on history and political science. There were also courses in math, physics, calculus, basic algebra, differential equations, and everything in between. They even offered specialized courses in astrophysics, anthropology, animal husbandry, auto mechanics, social studies, electronics, small boat handling and navigation, bee-keeping, cuts of meat, and wine selection. Joe Crecca taught classical music, which he instructed by humming or whistling themes.[5] John McCain taught a social studies class called "The History of the World from the Beginning."[6] They had exams and grades, and even extra tutoring for those who needed it. They used the concrete floor as a chalkboard, with a broken piece of roof tile for chalk.

In the afternoons they took a siesta, and in the evenings they enjoyed book and movie reviews, and games. Backgammon was the most popular. They scratched a backgammon board on the concrete slab, scrounging toilet paper to make moving pieces. Their dice they made from soap. Another popular game option was bridge, using cards made from toilet paper. Jim had never played bridge before in his life, but he became quite good. The cards were too flimsy to be shuffled in the usual way, but they sufficed. Towards the end of their imprisonment, and after much lobbying, the POWs landed a few decks of real playing cards. These were prized possessions, and each room treated its few decks with great care. After that, they played bridge every night and had big tournaments once a week. They stuck with the same partner all the time and made up bidding conventions.

Jim got to be quite the astute bridge player. After his return to the U.S., though, he never played again.

The men continued to receive occasional care packages. The most salvageable item, after the packages went through the V's hands, was freeze dried instant coffee—a wonderful treat when they got it. Eventually, a few thoroughly inspected socks and T-shirts made it through as well. Books sent in the care packages were never permitted. Towards the end the North Vietnamese did scrounge up a few English books from their own country, which they allowed to be passed around the camps. Most of them were English editions of a Russian book that had been approved by the Russian hierarchy. Still, the men were grateful for what they could get.

UPRISING

As time dragged on, the prisoners found their greatest source of strength in their faith—faith in their country and faith in God. Now consolidated at Hanoi, they discovered that there truly is strength in numbers. Living all together now in one camp, the prisoners developed a powerful unity. Up until this point, the most senior ranking American officials had been isolated in the Hilton, unable to contact the rest of the prisoners. Now they had an opportunity to organize their men and exercise the privileges of their rank.

In strict violation of the rules, Brigadier General Robinson Risner, senior officer at the camp, set up a church service. The men who wanted to participate wrote out hymns on toilet paper and joined together in songs of praise. As they were singing, the guards burst in and grabbed Risner to take him back to solitary confinement. But the presence of God filled the room, emboldening the prisoners, and instead of sitting down and shutting up, they sang louder. As Risner was led away for punishment, he heard a familiar refrain resounding though the camp:

> Oh, say can you see by the dawn's early light
> What so proudly we hailed at the twilight's last gleaming?
> Whose broad stripes and bright stars thru the perilous
>   fight,
> O'er the ramparts we watched were so gallantly streaming?
> And the rocket's red glare, the bombs bursting in air,
> Gave proof through the night that our flag was still there.
> Oh, say does that star-spangled banner yet wave
> O'er the land of the free and the home of the brave?

Years later, Robinson "Robbie" Risner told reporters that pride in his men singing the National Anthem as the V led him away for torture made him "feel nine feet tall and as though he could have gone bear hunting with a switch."[7] In 2001 the Air Force Academy installed a statue of Risner as a tribute to his bravery. It is nine feet tall, and in his hand he is clutching a switch.

Singing their national anthem boldly, the prisoners remembered why they were there: they were serving a nation strong, glorious, and free. They kept on singing loud and clear, even as the guards returned with ropes. One guard spat in the face of a prisoner, threatening punishment if they didn't shut up instantly.

The prisoner courageously replied, "Go ahead. You can drag us away one by one until there is only one man left. And that one man will still be singing." His defiance marked a turning point. The V backed off. Every night after that, the men who wanted to had a church service.[8]

MIKE'S FLAG

Standing in line for his weekly bath one day, a prisoner named Mike Christian, a young Naval pilot, spotted a tattered handkerchief lying in a gutter. He somehow managed to hide it from the guards and snuck it back into his cell, where he proceeded to turn the grimy cloth into an American flag. His cellmates donated slivers of their coveted soap so he could wash the fabric clean. Over the next few days they stole whatever they could get their hands on to help him with his project.

Mike worked on his flag every night. He ground up broken roof tiles to make red dye, using a tiny bit of ink and a sticky paste made out of water and rice. He took a piece of bamboo and turned it into a sewing needle to fasten little stars with a piece of blue thread from his blanket. When it was done, Mike held up his treasure, waving it proudly. The homemade flag had a profound effect on his cellmates. They stood at attention and saluted, many with tears in their eyes. From then on he brought it out once every day so the POWs in his cell could salute it and recite "The Pledge of Allegiance."

Then it happened. The guards found Mike's flag during one of their routine searches. About once a week they stripped the prisoners and made them run outside while the guards searched their clothing and their rooms. They came back for Mike that night. The beating started before they had even dragged him away. They wanted to make a lesson out of him. They took him to the torture room and beat him the entire night.

His cellmates awoke around sun-up the next morning, as Mike was roughly deposited back in the cell. They had beaten him almost to death. He had broken ribs, both eardrums were busted, and although his cellmates rallied around and tried to talk to him, Mike could not respond. His voice box had been crushed.

They broke his body but they couldn't break his spirit. Somehow, Mike managed to scrounge up another scrap of cloth. Within two weeks his cellmates found him working quietly in the corner of the cell, diligently creating another flag.[9]

JOHN McCAIN

Great faith and a fighting spirit rose in another prisoner who spent the majority of his five-and-a-half years of captivity away from the rest of the prisoners. John McCain, son of Admiral John Sidney "Jack" McCain Jr., who was commander of U.S. Forces in the Pacific, suffered in solitary confinement because he refused to comply with North Vietnamese requests for an apology and declined to issue a statement saying he was grateful for the treatment he had received from his captors. Because of his father, McCain was considered an especially valuable pawn. But McCain refused to play along. As a consequence, he was beaten every two to three hours for four straight days until his left arm, initially broken when he bailed out of his plane, was re-broken and his ribs were cracked.[10]

He was starved to one hundred pounds and had multiple limbs broken so badly they would require corrective surgery, but it was the lack of communication with his fellow prisoners that affected McCain the most. McCain would risk a beating any chance he got to communicate with someone outside of his cell. For all the prisoners, having a cellmate made the difference between being able to resist or not. Men with cellmates could depend on each other for morale, help when they were sick or weak from torture, talking, or just giving one another advice. With no one else to talk to, McCain relied heavily on prayer and on God's grace for his daily survival.

In the midst of his suffering, McCain prayed fervently for comfort, sometimes receiving relief from physical pain. He felt that God was making His presence known to him in various ways. One day, they moved him to a different cell, where he discovered the words, "I believe in God, the Father Almighty" scratched into the wall. Another time, McCain found himself wishing he could die rather than bear another minute of pain, after his captors had beaten him severely and tied him with ropes. Suddenly, a guard entered his cell and silently loosened the ropes that pinned his head between his legs. Four hours later, at the end of his watch, the same guard returned and tightened them again.

A few months later, on Christmas Day, McCain was allowed to stand in the sun for a short time. Across the courtyard, he caught the eye of the same guard who had loosened his ropes. The guard walked over to him and traced a cross in the dirt without uttering a word. Then he rubbed away the cross with his sandal and walked away. It was an experience McCain would hold onto for the rest of his life. Whatever happened to him, no matter how dark his circumstances, God would get him through.[11]

Chapter 14

Welcome to the Jungle

North Vietnam

May–December 1972

"And the rocket's red glare, the bombs bursting in air, gave proof through the night—that our flag was still there…"

—Francis Scott Key

I n May 1972, the guards burst into their cells in the middle of the night, forced them to roll up their mats, handcuffed them in pairs, and shoved 209 bewildered prisoners, including Jim, into the back of army trucks. An armed guard sat with them to make sure they didn't try to talk or lift up the canvas to look outside. It turned out to be a miserable two-day trip, and the prisoners were never allowed out, even for bathroom breaks. Squeezed like sardines in the back of the truck, they were forced to pass a bucket around to relieve themselves. One poor guy froze up in front of the others. The other men closed their eyes and turned their heads, but he was unable to go and suffered excruciating pain for the entire trip.

After two wretched days and nights of travel, the prisoners disembarked in the middle of a dense, misty jungle, facing a walled compound of dungeon-like cells carved out of rock. They called it the Dogpatch, and it was the worst prison any of them had occupied thus far. The cramped, dingy cells had not been occupied for many years, and vermin had moved in. The men were used to sharing their space with rats, but here they encountered something far worse: snakes. One prisoner entered his new cell only to be greeted by a cobra ready to strike.

During the rainy season, which is May through October in Northern Vietnam, several inches of water covered the floors of the buildings. The prisoners' clothes mildewed due to the constant damp conditions. The cells here had no windows, only tiny ventilation holes, and there was no electricity. On the one hand this worked out in their favor: they could actually sleep without a glaring light bulb in their faces for the first time during their imprisonment. Their beds consisted of wooden planks. Jim found himself sleeping more than ever once he got locked in the Dogpatch.

There was one improvement at the Dogpatch, though: after five years of pumpkin soup, the prisoners enjoyed corn mixed in with their rice, and every morning they had sweet hot milk. Unfortunately, the food was sparing, given out only twice a day. They would later learn that the improvement in diet was intentional. Now they were being fattened up for release. But their homecoming was still several months away.

Dogpatch was in the mountains, 105 miles north-northeast of Hanoi, in the no-fly zone between North Vietnam and China. About half of the total prison populace had been moved there, while the rest remained in the Hilton. One reason for this move was likely to disrupt the U.S. POW organization which by now had become very strong at the Hilton. Additionally, the men figured out later that the North Vietnamese were fairly certain Nixon was going to send in the heavy artillery and B-52s against Hanoi. The V wanted to protect their "investment" by hiding some of the POWs in the jungle, in case some errant bombs hit the Hanoi Hilton. They wanted to be sure they had some surviving prisoners to bargain with.

At Dogpatch the prisoners never left their cells. Sitting in the dark for eight wretched months with nothing but time on their hands, they occupied themselves making ingenuous crafts that would have impressed Martha Stewart. They made candles for themselves out of lard, which provided a little light. They made the candles by skimming the tiny tabs of pork fat floating in their soup, and saving it in a dish fashioned out of a lead toothpaste tube. Using the drawstring from one of their garments as a wick, and lighting it with the cigarette from their nightly smoke, the men enjoyed an occasional lighted evening. They also tried to make booze from fermented rice, but it didn't work out. Instead of fermenting the rice just rotted.

It was miserably dark almost all the time, increasing the men's boredom and desperation to get out. Once Jim and his cellmate, who he described as a skinny Naval pilot with a southern drawl, watched through a hole in the rock wall of their cell as some young North Vietnamese guards took turns pretending to drive an old dilapidated Jeep. One guard would sit in the driver's seat, trying to get it to move, while a few others pushed it from behind. The vehicle wouldn't budge. After enjoying this scene for several days, Jim and his cellmate hatched a plan to get out of prison for a while and have a little fun. They conned the guards into letting them out by promising that they would get the Jeep started. The guards had been trying to start it with the car in gear and the clutch disengaged, meaning they were trying to push against the transmission. They had no idea how to drive a manual transmission. Jim hopped into the driver's seat and depressed the clutch to get the Jeep started, while his cellmate distracted the guards. The Jeep rolled forward, and the guards whooped and hollered excitedly. Now it was their turn, but they hadn't seen Jim depress the clutch, so they still had no idea how to make the car move. They replayed the scene several times. Jim would start the Jeep and get it to move a few feet, then the guards would attempt it, and the car wouldn't budge. Jim kept shrugging his shoulders and pretending he had no idea what was wrong. The guards' initial excitement turned into frustration—which they took out on the prisoners. Jim and his cellmate paid for their bit of fun with a severe beating.

After eight miserable months, in January 1973, 208 prisoners returned to Hanoi in a bumpy two-day drive through the mountains. One of the prisoners, Marine WO John Frederick, had died, presumably of typhoid fever, while confined at Dogpatch. As they jostled along the winding mountain roads, the prisoners noticed a dramatic change in their treatment. The guards were much more relaxed now. They didn't handcuff the prisoners together, and they even allowed them to peek under the canvas to see where they were going. As they drew nearer to Hanoi, the prisoners saw for themselves what accounted for the change. The city had been destroyed. While they had been safely ensconced in the mountains, American B-52s had, in Jim's words, "bombed the shit out of Hanoi." There was almost nothing left.

The prisoners stared in shock at the mass destruction of the city, and then looked back at each other, wide-eyed. They couldn't speak, but they didn't have to. Every one of them was thinking the same thing. The war must be over, or very nearly.

Freedom was in sight.

Chapter 15

Operation Homecoming

Hanoi, North Vietnam

January–April 1973

"Imagine you're imprisoned in a cage; imagine the cage surrounded by the smell of feces; imagine the rotted food you eat is so infested with insects that to eat only a few is a blessing; imagine knowing your life could be taken by one of your captors on a whim at any moment; imagine you are subjected to mental and physical torture designed to break not bones but instead spirit on a daily basis. That was being a prisoner of North Vietnam. Then imagine one day, after seemingly endless disappointment, you are given a change of clothes and lined up to watch an American plane land to return you home. That was Operation Homecoming."
—Andrew H. Lipps, *Operation Homecoming: The Return of American POWs from Vietnam*[1]

The Hilton was abuzz with the news. The prisoners who had been left behind filled in the POWs returning from the Dogpatch on everything they had missed. It had been especially eventful in the last month and a half. It had been a nightly drama for the POWs at the Hilton, watching the sky light up with bombs and missiles as American B-52s blew the city of Hanoi to pieces.

The Nixon administration had launched the air campaign, dubbed "The Christmas Bombing" or "Operation Linebacker" on December 18, 1972, in response to stalled and "tortuous" negotiations with North Vietnam. The bombing went on for twelve days, during which the U.S. dropped almost forty thousand tons of bombs on the almost completely evacuated city of Hanoi.[2]

Not long after, for the first time since their imprisonment, the prisoners were led out into the courtyard all at once and ordered to organize according to military rank. A North Vietnamese official then read to them, in broken English, the entire text of the Peace Accord that had been signed in Paris on January 23, 1973, ending the war.[3] It took a really long time to read, and when he finally got to the part about the prisoners being released, no one reacted. Jim felt sure the V expected cheering and rowdy celebration, but the men simply returned to their rooms, sat on their concrete bunks, and waited. After years of enduring one disappointment after another, they couldn't feel excited about the promise of release. They were afraid to hope again. No one could be certain the release would really happen. The sick and wounded soldiers were to be released first. After them, the prisoners would be released in groups, in order of capture. They had no idea when the first group would be released, or how long it would be between groups.

The prisoners were on edge, scared the V would not honor the agreement, or that something terrible would happen to spoil everything. The next two weeks were a nerve-wracking, gut-wrenching time. The prisoners continued in their daily routine as they had for years, trapped, waiting, and in a constant state of agitation. Finally, on February 12, 1973, forty sick and wounded POWs were bussed from the camp and taken to Hanoi's Gia Lam Airport, where U.S. officers waited to accompany them home.

The prisoners' return to freedom had finally begun.

RELEASE PROTEST

A few days after the first prisoners left, Jim and nineteen other men were taken to the other side of the camp, where the sick and wounded had been taken the night before their release. The V handed them each a set of new clothes, a grey "uniform" especially designed to make it look like they had dressed the prisoners well while they were in custody.

Their captors told them, "You are going to be released tomorrow."

The prisoners were dumbfounded. They expected to be released in order of capture, and this was definitely out of order. The selected group of twenty men refused to leave. Their senior ranking officer acted as spokesperson for the group.

"It has always been our policy that we will go in the order of shoot-down. You have already released the sick and wounded, but now it is supposed to be in order of the longest held prisoners. This is not right, and we won't go."

The North Vietnamese refused to budge. This was the way it was going to be, they informed the POWs. But Jim and the rest of his group were adamant. They told the Vietnamese that they would have to carry them onto the planes—they would not go unless it was in the exact order of captivity. The discussions continued that way virtually all night. Occasionally the North Vietnamese would get up and leave the room, returning later only to reiterate their orders.

Finally, an American Air Force colonel in his dress blues entered the room. He had accompanied Henry Kissinger to Hanoi to sign the final agreements, and the V had apparently retrieved him to settle the dispute. He told the men that their out-of-order release had been worked out in a side deal. There had been some last-minute problems with the negotiations, and Kissinger was in Hanoi trying to work them out. Releasing these twenty men out of order was a goodwill offering on the part of the Vietnamese—the U.S. could not dictate the terms.

The prisoners still refused to go out of order. Exasperated, the colonel asked, "Well, do you still obey direct orders from your military?"

The men replied, "Yes."

The colonel snapped, "Then I am *ordering* you to get on that plane tomorrow!"

FEBRUARY 18, 1973

Jim never knew why he had been selected to leave in that special group of twenty men, later dubbed "Kissinger's Twenty." The other prisoners were to be released in groups of one hundred. Exhausted by the all-night negotiations, Jim took off his prison pajamas for the last time, and put on his new uniform. In his words, "It was hard to believe at first. We got on the bus and drove to Gia Lam Airport—of course, we were all just gawking around, because it was the first time we'd seen Hanoi, really, since we'd been there. And the destruction was really evident. Lots of people were watching—it was kind of a big deal for them, too, I guess."[4]

Arriving at Hanoi's Gia Lam Airport, they saw droves of North Vietnamese citizens who had come out to witness their departure. The Paris Peace Accord included detailed instructions on the procedure for turning the POWs back over to their country. The men formed two lines and were returned to their country one at a time. A Vietnamese official and an American would call off the same name, and the man being released would step forward to be met by an American officer, who escorted him to the C-141 Starlifter. Naval POWs were met by a Naval officer, Air Force was met by Air Force, and in this fashion each POW received his own traveling companion.

From February 12 through April 1, 1973, a continual flow of flights out of Hanoi returned 591 POWs to American soil and to their anxiously awaiting families. According to the U.S. Department of Defense, 325 Air Force personnel, 77 Army, 138 Navy, 26 Marines, and 25 civilian employees of U.S. government agencies were returned. Tragically, many thousands never came home. According to the National Archives, 58,220 United States military personnel lost their lives in the Vietnam War. As of June 9, 2016, according to the Defense POW/MIA Accounting Agency, 1,618 Americans are still missing in action and unaccounted for in Southeast Asia and China.[5]

Jim waited his turn in line, still in disbelief, for them to call his name: "Captain James Richard Shively." He stepped forward. It wasn't a dream. He was going home.

Part Three

Home Again

ONE MORE ROLL

We toast our hearty comrades

Who have fallen from the skies,

And were gently caught by God's own hands

To be with Him on high.

To dwell among the soaring clouds

They've known so well before,

From victory roll to tail chase

At heaven's very door.

As we fly among them there

We're sure to hear their plea,

Take care my friend, watch your six,

And do one more roll for me.

—Commander Jerry Coffee in Hanoi, 1968

Chapter 16

Return to Freedom

Clark Air Force Base, Philippines

Travis Air Force Base, Solano County, California

February–April 1973

t wasn't until the plane was actually airborne that Jim decided it was, in his words, "for real." Celebration broke out as the Star-lifter ascended and flew across the coast.

In the words of Ed Mechenbier, a fellow POW and friend of Jim's for life, "When we got airborne and the frailty of being a POW turned into the reality of freedom, we yelled, cried and cheered."[1]

According to another POW, "Everything seemed like heaven.[2] When the doors of that C-141 closed, there were tears in the eyes of every man aboard."

Aeromedical teams tended to them during the two-and-a-half hour flight, while the men smoked and laughed and got caught up on the topics of the day.

They were pleasantly surprised but unprepared for the heroes' welcome they received at Clark Air Force Base in the Philippines. After years of subhuman treatment, suddenly they found themselves received like royalty, with television cameras, flashing lights, cheering crowds, and requests for interview after interview.

Initially, the repatriated POWs suffered apprehension about their return home. They had no idea what kind of welcome they would receive back in the United States. The officers accompanying them quickly set their minds at ease. The American people were glued to their TV sets, anxiously awaiting their homecoming. As the men deplaned one by one in the Philippines, they were asked to go straight to the TV cameras and "say a few words" to the excited Americans watching over the live broadcast. It started to sink in for Jim when his feet touched the ground on the red carpet that had been rolled out for their return. He was free. Smiling, he saluted the welcoming officers, waved at the crowds, and spoke a few words of appreciation into the microphone.

It was all a whirl.

Finally, after the speeches and interviews were over, they drove the POWs to the hospital for a brief physical to determine if they were healthy enough to travel home. Jim found himself deposited in a nice, clean room. He had a bed—with sheets—and took a long, hot shower. A tailor came in and measured him. He had to have a couple of fittings for a new uniform with ribbons, as the men were supposed to look nice when they got back to the States. The chefs on base had prepared a soft diet for the men, unsure of their physical condition, but most of them bypassed the soft food and headed straight for the steak. Jim ate his first real meal in years: steak, eggs, and hash browns.

Jim and several others took time to visit the schools on base. The students couldn't wait to welcome the returning patriots with hand-made signs. "God Bless America and You," read one poster. When the men arrived at the middle school, the nine hundred excited students waiting outside became so unmanageable the teachers had to move everyone indoors. Jim gave a short talk and thanked the kids for their hearty welcome. One young man had a very special gift for Jim: it was the bracelet he had worn while Jim was in prison, engraved with Jim's name and shoot-down date. It had been worn so much it broke in half, so the student had had another bracelet hastily made for Jim, etched with the date of his release: February 18, 1973.[3] For the rest of his life, Jim would make middle school kids a priority on his speaking schedule.

Jim's nurse had flown in from Fairchild Air Force Base in Spokane. She filled him in on the upcoming Expo '74, and on the POW bracelets that so many in Spokane were wearing in his honor.[4] Jim was humbled and pleased. He took another really long, really hot shower, and then was whisked away to the dentist for several fillings.

One of Kissinger's Twenty had been whisked out of Clark early due to a family emergency. Another stayed behind to be treated.

Joe Crecca had received devastating news upon his arrival at Clark. The camp authorities had withheld his mail, so he had no idea that his father had passed away in 1968 and his wife had divorced him a year before. He was, in his words, "an emotional wreck," and the Air Force decided that it was "inadvisable" for him to travel. His nurse sat with him as he sobbed and took some extra days to recover. His flight surgeon released him to return to the States on February 23.

The remaining eighteen men boarded a C-141 Starlifter bound for Honolulu. As the men stepped out onto the red carpet and saluted the attending officers, Jim broke away briefly to hug two young teenagers who had been waiting to tell him goodbye. It was a sweet gesture. He was rewarded with a bag of cookies and one-half of a bracelet. The wearer, Susan, wanted to keep the other half for herself.[5]

SPOKANE, WA

On February 18, the telephone rang, shocking Harold and Jeanette awake. Jeanette looked at the clock—it was 1:30 in the morning. The United States Air Force was calling to inform them that Jim was on a plane bound for Clark Air Force Base. She hung up the phone and shouted for Harold to start packing. Two days later, Harold, Jeanette, and Phyllis were on a military flight out of Fairchild, headed for San Francisco.

Jim slept through the flight to Hickam Air Force Base in Honolulu. After refueling and a celebration for the POWs, he climbed back
onto the plane and fell asleep again.

Hours later, someone shook him awake. It took a while for his
thoughts to come together. They were preparing to land in the States.
The POWs would each be returned to the major Air Force hospital
nearest their home, and Jim's was the David Grant Medical Center at
Travis Air Force Base. He watched out the plane window as they
descended into the sunny San Francisco Bay area. It was a beautiful
day.

The Shively family waited impatiently on the red carpet that had
been rolled out to welcome the eighteen returning patriots. With them
was a considerable "fan club," eight hundred strong, waving banners
and applauding as the plane touched down and the returning veterans
stepped out.[6]

Jeanette could not contain herself long enough for Jim to walk
the length of the carpet. Almost as soon as he disembarked, she broke
away from the crowd and ran to embrace him. It was an emotional
planeside reunion, lacking words but not lacking tears.[7] Jim greeted
his family with hugs, still feeling like he must be in a dream. He saw
a banner in the crowd, "Welcome Home, Captain James R. Shively—
Spokane's Finest!" A woman stepped out of the crowd and thrust a
loaf of banana nut bread at him. She had made it specially for "her
man." Others, too, showered him with presents and showed off their
bracelets with his name on them.

The family barely had time to reunite before a government official whisked Jim off to the doctor for a more comprehensive physical, followed by an intelligence debriefing. He was ushered to a special, secured wing of the hospital, away from the crowds and the press. Physically, he was better off than many. He had lost nearly fifty pounds, but that would quickly be remedied by his mother's southern-fried cooking. He also would eventually need a whole new set of upper teeth.

He did suffer some more severe long-term physical complications. His nerves had been so damaged by the torture that he could not feel pain in certain areas of his body, like parts of his hands and arms. Once, later in his life, he punctured himself with a nail while setting up a dock. He had no idea until he saw his blood in the water around him. Another time the hood of a car slammed on his hand and actually latched, but he never felt it.

His biggest long-term physical problem was boils, the same problem that had plagued him throughout his imprisonment. These would require multiple trips to the ER long after his release, and they never totally went away. By the time he reached America, the boils under his arms were so bad that he could hardly put his arms down. He had to undergo minor surgery to have them lanced. The doctors explained the cause of his unusual condition: he had smaller-than-normal pores. In fact, they took pictures of him for research because they had never seen a case of clogged pores as bad as his. Years later, Jim joked that his gigantic boils made medical history, and he only hoped they had blacked out his face before publishing the photos in their research journals.

The returned POWs had to meet with a psychiatrist several times to assess their mental state before receiving clearance to leave the base. Jim thought the exams to test his mental acuity were silly, but he complied and was given a clean bill of mental health. A debriefing officer was assigned personally to him to help process his experience. Jim liked that he only had to discuss his time in captivity with one guy, and he built a good rapport with his officer, who didn't force him to talk and allowed him to debrief at his own pace. For the rest of his life, Jim adopted this method of talking about his war experiences. When people asked him questions, he complied with answers—if he felt like it.

Jim remained in the hospital at Travis for a few weeks. Like the rest of the prisoners, he was not allowed to leave the hospital until every trace of intestinal parasites had been cleared out of his body. His family stayed on the base for about a week, soaking in as much time as they could with him between his various medical appointments and press interviews.

After his family returned to Spokane to wait for Jim to come home, he received a phone call from Patsy Chambers, the sister of his old girlfriend, Nancy Banta, inviting him to join her family for dinner. She and her husband Leo had moved from Spokane to the San Francisco area, not far from the Base. He gladly accepted. When Patsy opened her door to welcome Jim, instead of responding to her welcoming hug he bowed, eyes on the ground, then quickly straightened up and apologized. He explained, embarrassed, that it was force of habit. Patsy had spent all day in the kitchen preparing an elaborate welcome-home meal. She asked him later what food he had missed the most while in Vietnam, and couldn't help chuckling at his answer. "Cheeseburgers and French fries" was the quick reply.

Jim quickly discovered that being a returned Vietnam POW catapulted him to star status. Once Patsy and her husband took him to dinner at the Fairmont Hotel in San Francisco, to see Trini Lopez. They met the actor George Kennedy, who invited them to join him at a local club to celebrate the premiere of his new movie. It turned out to be a star-studded event, including the mayor of San Francisco and Willie Brown, a California assemblyman at the time. But the biggest star of the night was Jim Shively. Champagne bottles overflowed their table, and Jim got up to make a speech. The movie premiere was for *Lost Horizon*, a musical about a fictional paradise called Shangri-La. Jim told the crowd, "Coming home to America is my Shangri-La!" The crowd gave him a standing ovation.

Jim got together several times with Patsy and her family while he was recovering at Travis. Neither of them had any idea that in the not-too-distant-future they would be in-laws. However, Patsy recalled later that "he talked about Nancy the whole time."

Memories and habits built up during his time in the prison camps that would follow Jim wherever he went. The night of the movie premiere, Jim stayed at Patsy's house, and Patsy shut his bedroom door so her children wouldn't disturb him in the morning. The next morning she saw Jim's door was wide open. At breakfast, Jim had an odd request for her: "Patsy, please don't shut my door." After all those years in confinement, he couldn't stand being shut up in a small room with a closed door.[8]

Chapter 17

Life in the Spotlight

Spokane, Washington

1973–1974

The returned POWs needed some time to adjust to their new lives in the States. The dreary prison cells and terrible treatment were far behind them—but their sudden climb to fame posed a unique challenge. Jim longed for peace and quiet, but there was little to be found.

He found he couldn't leave the house without causing a scene. Once he was in a bar in downtown Spokane with his friends Bob and Lois Banta. They had opted for a quiet table in the corner, but privacy was not to be had. Someone had recognized Jim, and before he knew it the entertainer on stage announced that there was a hero in the house. Jim found himself literally in the spotlight, which flashed from the stage to his table. In an instant, he was stripped down to his shorts on the back of a Vietnamese truck, being paraded through the streets of Hanoi in his underwear, surrounded by angry crowds and armed guards. Gracious as ever, Jim brushed the memory away and stood up to make a speech of thanks.

Jim hadn't counted on the notoriety that came with being a local hero. Once he arrived home in Spokane, his phone rang off the hook. Reporters pursued him constantly, and his picture was often in the paper, so even people who didn't know him felt as if they did. Everywhere he went well-meaning folks hounded him. Letters and bracelets came in from around the country. Jim was grateful for the accolades and support, but being a quiet and humble person by nature, he found it all hard to handle. He started going miles out of his way for simple errands, driving clear across town to buy cigarettes. But no matter where he went, people recognized him.

Besides being a local hero, Jim had a natural charisma in front of the microphone. He spoke with humility and wit, and somehow even managed to relay stories about the war with humor. The invitations for speaking engagements poured in, until they became virtually unmanageable. From the Rotary Club and local schools to the Police Guild, Boy Scouts, and Lions' Club, everyone wanted Jim, either to have him speak or to honor him with a ceremony. Jim, grateful for the public support, fielded all of this attention with composure and resilience—but eventually the intense pressure got to be too much.[1]

While in prison, one of his mental escapes had been planning the details of various trips he would take when he got out. He decided to make good on some of those dreams. He traveled to Tahiti, where he relaxed on the undeveloped and largely unpopulated island of Moorea. The island provided exactly the solitude Jim craved. He intended to stay for one week, but ended up staying for a month. After Tahiti, he went to Hawaii, Miami, and Boston.

The Air Force didn't seem to care much about how quickly he came back to work, and in fact he had about six months leave time built up, so he was in no rush. Ford Motor Company had given each of the POWs a year's free lease on a car, so Jim chose a Crown Victoria and hit the road again—this time taking his parents on a trip down south to visit relatives in Colorado, Kansas, and Texas.

PARTY AT THE WHITE HOUSE

"I speak for all the American people when I say never was the White House more proud than with the guests we have tonight."

President Nixon opened up the gala affair on May 24, 1973, with those words, thanking the assembled former POWs for their courage and bravery. It was an unprecedented show of hospitality at the White House, with 1,300 guests comprising the largest dinner ever in White House history.[2] Under gilded chandeliers, the president and first lady hosted the black-tie banquet in a gigantic red-and-yellow tent pitched on the White House lawn. The men looked snappy in their dress uniforms, vastly different from the haggard and gaunt released prisoners they had been when they last saw one another.

The reunions were powerful and emotional. John McCain and Ernest Brace had been housed in adjacent cells in the prison, forging a strong friendship through the only means of communication they had: tapping. The two men had never met face to face until this moment, and they threw their arms around each other.[3]

Bob Hope served as master of ceremonies, joking about his "captive audience," and promising that there would be no rice served with the meal.[4] Other big-name celebs like Jimmy Stewart, John Wayne, Sammy Davis Jr., Phyllis Diller, Joey Heatherton, Vic Damone, Edgar Bergen, and Irving Berlin were on hand to entertain and to celebrate with the POWs and their guests. Jim's table host was Edgar Bergen, a funny and gracious man. The guests were given gifts bearing the presidential seal—tie clasps for the men and brooches for the women. Jim met President Nixon and the First Lady, as well as Henry Kissinger. He was also excited to meet his favorite celebrity of the evening, Jimmy Stewart.

The party continued until the wee hours of the morning. The president informed the POWs that the White House was theirs for the night, and the staff rolled back the rugs on the second floor, where the guests danced and mingled as long as they wanted to. It was a fun and memorable evening for all. Perhaps the most moving part of the celebration was eighty-five-year-old Irving Berlin's performance of his classic, "God Bless America." Tears flowed freely as the guests stood and joined in the singing.[5]

RE-BLUING SCHOOL, MAXWELL AFB, MONTGOMERY, ALABAMA

Now Jim had to figure out what to do next. He had been offered a job at the Air Force Academy, teaching political science. It would mean a couple more years of school and a long-term military career, which Jim was not sure he wanted to pursue. In the winter of 1973, the Air Force offered a three-week "re-blueing" school for returning POWs in Montgomery, Alabama, designed to bring them up to speed on new Air Force policies, pay promotions, aircraft changes, and world developments. Jim's personnel officer talked him into attending—using Montgomery Air Base's beautiful golf course as bait. If he decided the classes weren't for him, Jim could get in a round of golf instead. Jim also had a prison mate, Ben Ringsdorf, whom he had befriended during his final years in the Hilton. Ben lived near the base in Alabama, so Jim went to check out the classes and visit Ben.

As it turned out, Jim was expected to attend every class session—and he learned the lesson the hard way. One afternoon he hit the golf course with some buddies, and a colonel hunted them down and ordered them back to the school. They obeyed, but Jim learned an important lesson about himself: he did not want people telling him what to do for the rest of his life. He did not want to control other people, either. After six years in prison, he knew all too well that life is too short to be so tightly regimented. He began to rethink his old dream of achieving high status in the Air Force. Maybe it was time to seek a new career.

RANDOLPH AFB, TEXAS

During the course of his travels Jim had opportunities to spend time with old prison buddies, which he always enjoyed and greatly looked forward to. They "got" each other like no one else could, and for the rest of his life he would attend POW reunions as often as he was able. It piqued his interest when he discovered that several former POWs were pursuing careers as commercial airline pilots.. He told his personnel officer he wanted to pursue a job with Eastern Airlines. Still hoping to keep Jim in the military, his personnel officer persuaded him to go to Randolph AFB, near San Antonio, Texas, thinking he would fall in love with flying fighters again. It had the opposite effect.

Flying the T-38, Jim discovered that he had gotten spoiled flying in combat. Flying drills at Randolph wasn't fun. They restricted his air space; he couldn't even do a loop without calling for clearance, and he felt like he was flying in a box. He made up his mind: it was time to do something else. He had lost six years in Vietnam, but now he had his life back, and he was going to live it his way, on his terms. He wanted to chart his own course.

He joined the staff at Fairchild Air Force Base to teach survival school for a few months, enough time to complete ten years of service. In June 1974 he retired from the Air Force and set out on an entirely new career path: he headed to law school.

Chapter 18

Don't Sweat the Small Stuff

"Any day you can turn the handle on the door and walk out of a room…is a good day."
—Captain James Richard Shively, 1942–2006

I n May 1976, Jim married his high school sweetheart, Nancy Banta.

Nancy had been married while Jim was still overseas and had two little girls, but her marriage was not a happy one. She and Jim reconnected in November 1975. Nancy said reuniting with Jim felt "safe, like when you come home after a long trip."

After thirty-four years as a bachelor, Jim suddenly found himself surrounded by females. Nancy's daughters, Amy and Jane, were five and ten months old when they got married, and two more baby girls followed soon after that, first Laura Ann, then Nicole Jeanette (Nikki).

Jim traded in his Porsche for a station wagon and sold his condo at a local ski hill to build a bigger house. He was a great dad, quickly becoming an expert at changing diapers, reading stories, and burping babies. He would often joke that he was just keeping a promise he made to himself while he was in prison: "When I finally get out of here, I will surround myself with beautiful females for the rest of my life."

SUCCESSFUL CAREER

Jim graduated from Gonzaga Law School and opened his own private practice in 1977. He rented an office in the Spokane Valley and hired an assistant. He survived on real estate closings, divorces, and criminal defense. Eventually, his practice grew to include six other attorneys, but Jim found he didn't care for the business side of owning a law firm. Just about the time he decided to leave private practice and pursue something else, a colleague told him about an opening at the U.S. Attorney's office.

It suited him perfectly. Jim found the variety of federal civil and criminal cases interesting and challenging, and he spent the next twenty years as an assistant U.S. attorney, eventually becoming a senior supervisor for the Eastern District of the Washington State Department of Justice, where he served for a time as acting U.S. Attorney. He became one of Spokane's top prosecutors, known around town for his integrity, his humility, his cool-headedness, and his ability to end almost every discussion with a laugh.[1]

Jim was an excellent trial lawyer, right from the start. He was brilliant with the law, but his natural charisma didn't hurt, either. The jury found his sense of humor and easy-going demeanor charming and engaging. During one of his first major trials, he found himself up against three of the most prestigious defense attorneys in Spokane. His brother-in-law, Bob Banta, happened to run into all three of them in an elevator on the first day of the trial, and asked them how it was going.

Their irritated reply: "That damn brother-in-law of yours...he opens his mouth and the jury falls in love with him on the first day! We don't have a chance."

Sure enough, Jim won the case.[2]

Jim was recruited repeatedly by the Democratic party to run for elected office, the first step in a plan to elect him to the U.S. Senate. He respectfully declined. He wanted to keep his focus on his family.[3]

FAMILY MAN

Jim was calm and collected, un-phased by the ups and downs that inevitably come with having four daughters. He also had a zest for life and loved to laugh, which meant Nancy and the girls were the targets of many pranks.

Once he wore a hideous clown mask to bed, then rolled over and tapped Nancy on the shoulder after she had crawled in next to him, sending her screaming and flying down the hallway. Another time when the younger girls wanted their ears pierced, Jim told them they were too young: if they got their ears pierced he would have to get his pierced, too. The next evening Jim strolled into the house after work wearing pearl earrings, shocking everyone present. It turned out the earring were magnetic, but rumor had already gotten around the neighborhood that Jim Shively had his ears pierced. Jim just chuckled.

It was difficult to get Jim riled up. He didn't get upset when the empty car, which someone had forgotten to put in park, rolled down the steep driveway and crashed into a tree. He didn't seem too distressed when one daughter brought home a "D" during her first semester of college, or when another snuck out of the house to a party and came home drunk. He had already lived through hell and survived. After Vietnam, his philosophy was that nothing in life was worth getting too worked up about.

He had a saying, "Don't sweat the small stuff—and it's all small stuff."

FIRE

After the war, Jim's ability to maintain a positive life outlook in the midst of life's traumas became a hallmark of his character. He rolled with whatever came his way—including a heart attack in 1982. He rarely complained or even acknowledged pain, but when he came in from working outside almost completely gray, Nancy rushed him to the emergency room where it was found that he had an almost total blockage. No surgery was required. In fact the blood to his heart had taken five different routes to get around the closure. The doctors said they had never seen anything like it. A few days later, Jim was up and about again. He was prescribed beta blockers and exercise at a rehabilitation center, but he hated them both. He quit the rehabilitation after three days, and, despite Nancy's protests, flushed the medicine down the toilet because it "slowed him down." The doctors were amazed, but Jim's heart had taken care of itself. He never had a heart problem again.

Jim's ability to look at life as a gift and to "not sweat the small stuff" also pulled him and his family through real tragedy. On October 16, 1991, a severe firestorm swept through their neighborhood and claimed the family home. One hundred and fourteen homes were lost that day, and one life. As the fires raged out of control, firefighters blocked off the entrances to the neighborhood. The Shivelys, who were at work and school, had no way of knowing if their home was still standing. The following day, after the smoke had cleared and the neighborhood reopened, they discovered a huge mound of charred, black rubble where their beautiful, custom-built home had been. Jim had designed it himself with the help of a family friend. It was the first and only time the girls saw their dad even come close to shedding a tear.

At first, they were afraid their two dogs, who had been in the garage, had died in the fire. Thankfully, a neighbor had captured the dogs as they were fleeing the home. Displaced and disoriented, the

Shively family stayed in a motel for about a month before finding a home to rent. Friends and family donated clothing for the girls and brought household goods until they could resituate.

The loss of their family home was devastating for Nancy. She missed the sentimental things like family pictures, the crafts the girls had made when they were young, Christmas ornaments, and the bracelet her dad had given her when she was ten. She was hospitalized and diagnosed with diabetes about a year later. She cited the stress of the fire, and the several subsequent moves, as triggers.

Jim's attitude was decidedly different. The disaster didn't seem to throw him off-kilter at all, which was hard for Nancy to understand at first. In her words, his overall attitude about the fire was that "shit happens." But Jim's strength and his calm, matter-of-fact demeanor held the family together. He refused to linger on painful situations or to allow self-pity. They could be thankful they were all alive, including the dogs, and they would start over and move on.

Ten years before the fire, Jim had commented, "There are certain times you think about it (Vietnam)...you think about the lessons you learned there, like setting your priorities. What I found out is that you don't need a lot of material things to be happy. I'm thankful for my family, my health, and my ability to come and go as I please."[4]

He had known real tragedy, and he was able to keep this challenge in perspective. A reporter interviewed him later about losing his home and most of his possessions, including his war medals. Jim's answer proved how deeply he had learned life's toughest lessons as a prisoner of war.

"I could have died that day over North Vietnam," he reflected. "But for some reason I didn't. Any day after that is a good day."[5]

But Jim did get his medals back. The following March, on his fiftieth birthday, it was standing room only as more than one hundred of Jim's friends and associates gathered for a surprise ceremony in the courthouse. Someone in the United States Attorney's office had organized the presentation, conducted by Speaker of the House Tom Foley. The Honorable Mr. Foley presented Jim with two Purple Hearts, two Silver Stars, one Bronze Star, one Distinguished Flying Cross, four Air Medals, and one Legion of Merit. The only war memento that could not be replaced was a pair of cufflinks given to Jim by President Nixon in 1973. Mr. Foley gave him a pair of Speaker of the House cufflinks instead, representing the third most powerful post in government.

Jim was modest, calling himself a survivor and not a hero. He jokingly chastised his officemates, telling the crowd, "I told people I would love to have my medals back, but I didn't want a big deal. Having the Speaker of the House (here) is kind of a big deal."[6]

After the fire, Jim and Nancy eventually rebuilt on their one-acre lot, happy to be back in their little corner of the world with their flower garden and their dogs.

LOSS

Jim remained in close contact with several of his prison mates, especially Mike Burns, Joe Crecca, and Loren Torkelson. After sharing such intense personal experiences, the men formed a very special brotherhood.

Torkelson was a burly Norwegian with a booming voice two octaves lower than most men. He had finished out the war a highly decorated officer, receiving two Silver Stars, three Flying Crosses, sixteen Air Medals, the Legion of Merit, the Bronze Star for Valor, the Meritorious Service Medal, and the Air Force Commendation Medal. When he came home from Vietnam, he earned a law degree and became a JAG Officer. He was only fifty-four when he died of a heart attack.

Jim attended the funeral with Joe Crecca and Bob Abbott, deeply saddened at the loss of their cellmate and "brother." Jim was not one to show emotion easily. At Loren's gravesite, Joe was crying openly. He knew Jim must feel the loss just as deeply, so he asked him why he wasn't crying. Somewhat bewildered by the question, Jim replied, "Because you're Italian and I'm not." Jim thought it a fitting testimony to what a great, lovable guy Loren was that several of his ex-wives were there to mourn him—plus a couple of current girlfriends.

Even more difficult for Jim was the loss of his family. In 1977, the same year Jim started his law practice, his mother died of cancer. His father had a heart attack and passed away very suddenly in 1980.

In September 1991, his only sibling, Phyllis, died of cancer, at the very young age of forty-six. Jim had started a journal that summer, stating on the first page that if he could discipline himself to write faithfully every day, he hoped it would turn into the book he had always dreamed of writing. On the day of Phyllis' funeral he wrote:

> It is difficult to believe that she is no longer here with us and that I am the only one of our little family remaining. One of life's little ironies that the one who chose the most dangerous profession and had people trying to kill me is the only one still surviving.[7]

Recording his thoughts about her death, he wrote that he wished he had told Phyllis he loved her before she became so sick. It was his last entry in that journal, and it would be fourteen years before he began a new one.

Chapter 19

Because You Cannot Hate and Live

J im never harbored anger or resentment about the war. He took full responsibility for his choices and his military career. In his heart of hearts, he was a fighter pilot. He had known the risk he was taking when he went to Southeast Asia to fly and to fight. He went for the adventure, for career advancement, and for the love of flying, fully aware of the potential consequences. He never blamed anyone else.

Jim was continually asked to speak at schools and other venues around Spokane, and complied several times a year. In an address to students at a local middle school, Jim once said,

There is no room in the vocabulary for failure—unless we let it in. Life isn't fair, it is only what you make of it. There is no failure—because each step you take, even if you fall down flat on your face—you learn something. I had the opportunity to be captured, the opportunity to be interrogated, the opportunity to be tortured and the experience of answering questions under torture. It was an extremely humiliating experience. I felt sorry for myself. I believed the world was supposed to be fair. The biggest lesson [I learned] is that the world is not fair. Once I learned that very hard, very slow lesson...I realized I could give up and die—or survive.[1]

Because he refused to be bitter, the war never fully got a grip on him. Once home, he certainly never forgot it, but it didn't destroy his life. His memories were never intrusive or debilitating.

If anything, his experiences shaped him for the better. The war had changed his priorities: early in his career he was highly ambitious to be chief of staff of the Air Force. He would have sacrificed virtually anything to achieve that goal. While in prison, he came to realize that other things, especially family, were far more important. He gave up those early aspirations for a simpler life.

He never regretted it.

BOBBY JOHNSTON

Some things that were important to other people were not impor-tant to Jim. He left private practice largely because he couldn't muster up concern for people's property line disputes, problems with neigh-bors, greedy divorces, and other issues he found trivial. One time, while a potential client rambled on about suing someone for some-thing Jim considered meaningless, Jim politely stood up, closed his briefcase, and walked out.

While Jim had a low tolerance for what he deemed petty lawsuits, he had an extreme soft spot for troubled veterans. He knew he was one of the lucky ones. Other Vietnam veterans were far less lucky in their lives after the war. Many suffered horribly from the trauma of their experiences, enduring mental and emotional breakdowns. One veteran occasionally showed up on Jim's doorstep, simply in need of an understanding ear. Jim fielded phone calls from families of vets who had read about him in the paper and needed his help. It was not uncommon for him to receive calls at home in the middle of the night, asking him to get someone's son out of jail for a DUI or bar fight. Jim always complied.

He also joined a veterans' support group as a mentor. Few could pay for his legal services, but Jim didn't care about that. Some men insisted on paying him in trade: lumber, shrubbery, an old car with no floor in it, and one time even a dog. One of those cases received national attention.

In 1982, Jim took on what would become the biggest trial case
of his early career, and the most significant to him. It involved his
defense of a Vietnam veteran named Bobby Johnston. Mr. Johnston
had fought in the war as a young Army man on the ground, experi-
encing the violence up close and personal. For years he had been
suffering from delayed stress syndrome and had actively sought psychiatric help from the Spokane Veterans Administration Medical
Center. According to Jim, he got nothing but a bottle of pills and a
bureaucratic runaround.

After years of torment and severe emotional and mental anguish,
Mr. Johnston snapped. He entered the VA facility with a gun and took
three health-care workers hostage.

Mr. Johnston was clearly guilty and Jim was advised by fellow
attorneys not to take the case. But after meeting with Bobby and
reviewing his medical history and the files from the VA, Jim came to
the conclusion that he had been severely misdiagnosed and mistreated.
He knew he had to take the case. At the trial, Jim argued that the
same government that willingly sent Bobby Johnston into the atrocities of war should have been just as willing to extend proper medical
care upon his return.

"Our country made a deal with those guys that we aren't living
up to," Jim stated in an interview.[2]

It was a very emotional and personal case for Jim, and he worked
on it tirelessly. He argued that only a perverted and unrealistic sense
of logic would conclude that every man could endure the horrifying

realities of war and come out whole. He knew, firsthand, many men who were strong, well-educated, and mentally sound going into the war, but came out broken and destroyed. He had lived with them in the prison camps, and he represented them at home.

According to Jim, many veterans were in urgent need of care—and they weren't getting it. Some could not hold down jobs or pay their bills. They could not submit to any kind of authority. Some who were committed, married men going into war ended up unable to maintain any type of close relationship after it ended. Some who had been clean and sober going in now depended on alcohol or drugs to forget the atrocities they had experienced. They got involved in the legal system by disturbing the peace or resisting arrest. Some who went into the war calm and mild-mannered returned anxious, angry, and reckless.

"There but for the grace of God go I" was Jim's realistic view. Jim knew that the line between hero and felon might be narrower than most people realize. Like many others, Bobby Johnston was a decent man, but he had been a victim of the system and improper care. Had he been treated with understanding instead of suspicion, it would have made all the difference for his mental health. Psychiatrists concurred, testifying that Mr. Johnston had no recollection of the hostage incident and was not responsible for his actions.[3]

After twenty hours of deliberation, the verdict came in. Jim and Nancy rushed down to the courtroom. It was a crushing blow: Mr. Johnston was found guilty.

Bobby thanked Jim for a job well done, but Jim was heartsick. In an interview following the verdict, he said simply, "It wasn't good enough."[4]

Later, Jim told a reporter that it worried him that the government refused to take any responsibility at all: "You know what the worst thing about losing that case was? It allows the community to avoid responsibility once again. We can say [Johnston's action] wasn't because of the Vietnam war, and it wasn't because of the Veterans Administration's poor treatment of him. It's not delayed stress, we can all tell ourselves. It's just that the guy is a bad character. We can say he did it because he doesn't handle anger and frustration in an acceptable manner."[5]

Jim pointed out that Bobby Johnston, now in treatment and under proper psychiatric care, was getting better. He was improving because he had admitted he had a problem that needed fixing. Jim said the government should do the same. Jim called what Johnston did, and why he did it, "evidence of our great national reluctance to deal with uncomfortable truths about war."[6]

Several jurors called Jim to say how sorry they were. One juror even wrote a letter to President Ronald Reagan expressing her outrage at the medical attention Bobby had not received. Even though he had lost, the trial generated attention, and Jim hoped it would be a catalyst for change.

His frustration and disappointment turned to joy three months later when Bobby's sentence was read. The judge could have given him twenty years to life. Instead, he gave Bobby a deferred sentence of ten years' probation, and a six-month suspended jail sentence.[7] Happiness reigned in the courtroom for Bobby and his family, who burst into thankful tears. Even Jim, usually so non-emotional, hid tears behind his smile. The final outcome of the trial was better than he had dared to hope for.

It was a landmark case for its time, and one of the first federal cases in history to provoke governmental response and awareness for veterans with delayed stress syndrome, now referred to as post-traumatic stress disorder (PTSD). Motivated by his personal, firsthand experience with the atrocities of war, Jim played an instrumental role in building national awareness of the kind of attention service men and women need when they return home from combat.

Chapter 20

The Last Battle

Spokane, Washington

2002–2006

O n the day of Phyllis' funeral, Jim had written, "When I die I want people to celebrate. I want everyone to remember that I enjoyed my time here, and had a wonderful, exciting life filled with great adventures."[1]

Jim was diagnosed with prostate cancer eleven years later, in 2002. True to form, he took it in stride. He had already lived longer than he ever expected to, and every day was a gift. For four years, he bravely underwent chemo and radiation. In January of 2006, he stopped the cancer treatments. They were extending his life but not bettering it.

It was a shock to everyone how quickly his condition deteriorated. The four girls were there to help Nancy with his care.

His old prison mate Mike Burns flew in from Florida, arriving just in time to share some final moments with his personal hero. Jim had not spoken or responded in days, but he seemed to be listening when Mike sat down to talk to him. Mike told him he still looked like a fighter pilot, and Jim's blue eyes, half-closed, sparkled.[2]

Oddly enough, Jim had predicted when his life would end. On their wedding day, someone had toasted Jim and Nancy: "Here's to fifty years of happiness!" Jim had quietly replied, "No, we will only be married for thirty years." His prediction, which struck Nancy as odd at the time, proved accurate. They enjoyed thirty years of marriage before cancer claimed his life.

February 18, 2006, was uncharacteristically bright. It was exactly thirty-three years since Jim's release from Vietnam. Now he would be freed from his cancer-stricken body. He died at 5:00 that morning, surrounded by his wife and daughters.

Friends and colleagues turned out by the hundreds to honor Jim Shively and to say goodbye. In a letter to another ex-POW, Jim's old prison mate Joe Crecca summed it up in moving words: "Anyone who knew Jim feels his loss like a dagger."[3]

TRIBUTE

Jim's friends and family turned out in droves for his funeral. Many of them spoke highly of him, expressing the deep loss everyone felt. Joe Crecca shared a moving address.

I've lost two of my best friends. First was Loren Torkelson. Now, I've lost you, too.

Jim, it's bad enough to lose someone you love. But it is an emotion most terrible to lose someone uniquely like you who I not only loved but liked, too. When we were cellmates you showed the rest of us how to live. You never said an angry word to any of us no matter how much we deserved it. And no angry words were ever spoken to you, either. When you suffered endless pain and discomfort, you never complained. In fact, you smiled. You showed us what real courage was.

Jim, these last few years you demonstrated your immense strength of character and your unbelievable courage in the face of overwhelming odds. We are all humbled by this and doubt that we could ever be your equal under similar circumstances. Jim, when we were cellmates you taught me so many things. You taught me Russian, politics, world history. But the biggest lesson I learned from you was how to live; how much better we ourselves would be if we were like Jim Shively. Remember the poem we read together? It was about soldiers in World War I. The last five lines of that poem are how I will bid my final farewell to you, dear Jim:

By your courage in tribulation,

By your cheerfulness before the dirty devices of this world,

You have won the love of those who have watched you.

All we remember is your living face,

And that we loved you for being of our clay and spirit.

Godspeed, Jim. If anyone deserves a place in Heaven, it is you.

Joe Crecca

March 3, 2006

TWO THOUSAND LUNCHES

One of Jim's best friends after the war was a colleague, Rolf Tangvald. Rolf wrote a moving account of their friendship, reflecting on their time together during weekly lunches for several years. Rolf considered Jim a great man, a loyal friend, and an exceptional attorney.

He asked if I wanted to get lunch. If I had realized that the person asking would become one of my closest friends, I certainly would have said yes. Instead, hoping to impress my new employers at the United

States Attorney's Office by working through lunch, I declined. Luckily, he asked me to lunch a few days later and I accepted. That lunch became one of over two thousand meals I enjoyed with Jim Shively over the next fifteen years.

Jim and I both worked as assistant United States Attorneys for the United States Department of Justice. The office was a fast-paced, high-anxiety workplace where everyone was expected to be at the top of their game at all times. If there was any room for criticism, the political types in the office were sure to let others know, often behind your back. Being only twenty-eight years old, I was a bit overwhelmed.

Jim was twenty-one years my senior. He was a part of my parents' generation, not mine. At first, I figured that Jim would be just another older attorney in the office that would find fault in the new kid. With a laugh, he called me the "FNG," a not-so-kind military term for the "new guy." However, it didn't take long to realize that there was something different about Jim. First, he didn't compete with others. Jim was comfortable knowing what he knew and not knowing what he didn't know. He was comfortable in his own skin. Second, Jim rarely got angry. Instead, it seemed that Jim had seen enough to know what was and what wasn't important. "Don't sweat the little stuff" was a frequent mantra. Third, Jim was nice to everyone, even those I later discovered he really didn't care for too much.

Two weeks into my career at the U.S. Attorney's Office, Jim's house burned down. All the way down. Nothing left. All of his family's possessions gone. He was very relieved that his wife and four daughters, as well as the family dog, were safe. While Jim was disappointed, he kept a remarkable spirit. During our lunches over the next year, Jim would update me on the rebuilding process, the status of his four daughters, and he continued to provide advice on how to best represent the United States.

Jim and I both initially worked on civil matters. This meant that we represented the United States' interests when it, or any of its agencies, were sued. As one might imagine, it was a big task. I was fortunate to have Jim's able counsel and guidance. During many of our lunch discussions, Jim would simply chuckle to himself when he found out how my "bull in a china shop" approach failed to get the results I expected. Instead, Jim taught me that representing a sovereign nation in litigation with its citizens is a sacred trust. The goal was not always to win. The goal was to always do justice. Similarly, when I handled criminal matters, Jim reminded me that my innate instinct to seek the maximum sentence in every case was a bit rigid. Instead, our obligation was to recommend an appropriate sentence that took into account not only the protection of the public but also the rehabilitation of the offender. Jim's professionalism in representing the United States became the standard by which I measured my work throughout my career.

Over the next decade and a half, Jim and I would discuss every conceivable topic during lunch. Politics, religion, our families, our upbringing, his tenure in Viet Nam, his shenanigans at the Air Force Academy, his cases, my cases, life philosophies, and much more were discussed over burgers, subs and salads. It is fair to say that Jim and I were on opposite ends of the political spectrum. However, when he told me that the local Democratic party was drafting him to run for Congress, I immediately volunteered to help him in any way possible. The reason was simple. Jim was a person of integrity. Even though we wouldn't always agree on the solution to an issue, I always knew that Jim would honestly try to work the issue, instead of simply playing politics with it.

Jim and I also came to the issue of faith from different perspectives. While Jim certainly did not place the same importance on faith that I did, he knew my beliefs were important to me. Instead of simply ending our conversations regarding faith or changing the subject, Jim engaged me and never took the easy "shots" that often are taken with respect to the issue. I admired Jim and appreciated that he didn't belittle my beliefs, but actually found value in me for having them.

While Jim and I started as peers in the U.S. Attorney's Office, over time, he was promoted. First, to civil chief. Then, to first assistant. Finally, to acting United States Attorney. I thought that Jim's elevation to supervising me, and ultimately to supervising everyone, might cause a strain on our friendship. It didn't. Frankly, Jim wouldn't let it. First, he never gave me any special access or knowledge into the operations of the office, even though I know he would have liked to have bounced some ideas back and forth before coming to a decision. This protocol turned out to be very important. Initially, it maintained a proper relationship between management (him) and employee (me).

Second, it allowed Jim to simply ignore the slings and arrows that came from others regarding my "access" to the boss. Third, we had more important things, like family and how proud he was of his daughters, to talk about.

Sometime around 2002, Jim and I were having a normal lunch when he told me that he had been diagnosed with prostate cancer. Immediately, my heart sank. However, I soon realized that nothing between Jim and I had changed. We were still each other's confidants and friends. Now, I had the honor of trying to help my friend by listening more and talking less. Jim's treatment first took him out of the office for extended periods. Ultimately, as the disease progressed, it took him from the office altogether. The disease's progression was unrelenting and sapped Jim's energy, but rarely his spirit. I was honored to continue weekly lunches with Jim throughout his ordeal. We talked about the disease. We talked about the fact that the options were dwindling. We talked about family and finances. Sometimes we talked about subjects that were mainly designed to provide a distraction from how poorly Jim felt. Jim even let me talk about faith, because he knew I had to.

Toward the end, Jim couldn't eat lunch any more. Instead, I would pick up a milkshake at Zips for Jim and we would continue as if nothing had changed. Thinking back, I am so thankful for even the difficult visits. It was during these lunches that I came to the realization of the uniqueness of our friendship. Even though Jim was quite ill, we both appreciated just feeling normal for a bit and talking like we had for the past fifteen years.

During the last week, Jim told me that he had discontinued treatment and that the disease would soon be fatal. I remember telling him that we both had known what the ultimate result was going to be for some time now. He smiled and agreed. His thoughts, naturally, during our last lunch were about his family and how he would miss them. He also shared with me that he had lived a great life and wasn't worried about what was coming. Remarkably, he even comforted me by sharing that he did have a faith and that, with a grin, I should quit worrying about him. This piece of information was, and continues to be, a comfort to me. We said goodbye to each other, lingering a bit because we both knew it would be for the last time. Jim died later that week.

Looking back, it is strange to think that the most abiding and most important part of my career were the hours I spent at lunch with my friend. Jim has now been gone for more than eight years. I think about him daily. I hear his voice in my head and I still chuckle about his sense of humor and the stories he told. I am thankful that I had the opportunity to have a close friendship with someone I respected so much. I wish we would have had time for a few more lunches.

Rolf Tangvald
October 2014

Epilogue

I t is hard to write a proper ending to the life story of a man who remains an enigma in so many ways. Jim Shively was a man of few words. I didn't get much instruction from him, in words, on how to live life well. But I learned a lot from his unspoken example. You could not be in the same room, let alone grow up in a home with Jim Shively and not be affected by his humor, wit, calm demeanor, honest character, and genuine humility.

He modeled for me what it looks like to have peace in all situations. His inner peace was never conditional upon his outward circumstances;

in fact, the strength he radiated calmed any storm. He was like a pearl that doesn't lose its shine when faced with adversity, but becomes more polished and rare because of it.

As an adult, I realize his influence on my life has been incalculable. I understand by Dad's example that life sends us fiery trials, and it's up to us to choose how to walk through them. We can adopt a crippling "victim" mentality, or we can face the fire head-on and come out the other side refined.

A few days before Dad died, I went into his room by myself and held his hand and prayed while he slept. "Dad," I whispered, "I just want you to go and be with Jesus."

Suddenly, his eyes popped open and he looked right at me. He said, "I will," and then he gave me a little smile and went back to sleep.

I don't think he ever woke up again after that. He died three days later. A little while after his death I dreamed I saw him in an immense, magnificent rose garden, clipping the flowers and smiling. I got the impression that he was at work tending the roses in God's royal garden.

Afterword

In Memoriam

"Jim and I were POWs in North Vietnam together. Jim was shot down in a flak suppression flight of F-105s on May 5, 1967. The F-105 was the assignment of choice out of pilot training. Either you had to be good or you had to be lucky to get a 105, because there were only a few assignments. Jim was good.

"I met Jim for the first time in September 1967. I say 'met,' but what I mean is that we were in adjacent cells and all we could do was talk to each other without actually seeing each other. Months later I was in the same cell with Jim and two other POWs, Loren Torkelson and Bob Abbott. Loren was our leader, Bob and I were the entertainment, and Jim was the stabilizing influence.

"When you are in the same room with the same guys for year after year where all—I repeat—*all*—the things you do in a day are in close quarters, you become family. You become brothers. Brothers forged of a common and very harsh experience; brothers in arms, brothers who endure the same hardships for years and years.

"Jim was a son, a brother, a husband, a father, a friend, and a hero. I have told others when speaking about Jim Shively that he was a prince of a man. I meant it then and I mean it now. Jim Shively was one of the best, one of the brightest, and he was a prince of a man. I am proud to have been his friend."

Joe Crecca, POW, North Vietnam, 1966–1973

"The ancient Greeks intoned that on rare occasions the gods gift us with a 'golden one,' a being of special grace and talents. If we are exceptionally fortunate in our lifetime, we may be blessed by knowing a person of uncommon valor and grace. Captain James R. Shively was such a man.

"Shively would courageously endure nearly six years of barbaric captivity in the infamous 'Hanoi Hilton.' The harsh character-strengthening anvil of his POW experience was, however, to forge a stronger man. The emaciated figure who emerged from his cell was even more steely than the brave young pilot who entered.

"As an attorney, his reputation was sterling. It would be a Herculean task to identify a more respected public official. His admirers are legion. And as a selfless volunteer mentor to high school and Gonzaga college students, and a regular guest speaker at Gonzaga University political science classes, he created a profound impact on his appreciative audiences. He literally and figuratively personified the noble code of 'Duty...Honor...Country.'

"Hollywood's pool of gifted screen writers would be unfairly challenged to draft a more inspiring script than that of Jim Shively's remarkable life."

Jerry Hughes, former Washington State senator, professor of political science at Gonzaga University

"I came to know Jim quite well at the Academy, and later, at Georgetown. After his release, it was a great surprise that he had no bitterness about the war, and absolutely no self-pity about the fact that he spent almost six years of his life as a POW, despite the deprivation, the torture, and the near starvation.

"In 1974, my wife and daughters and I were living in Washington, D.C., and I was working as an attorney at a law firm there—I had just graduated from Columbia Law School in 1973. I had not seen your father since we left Georgetown in February 1965. In February 1974 (or thereabouts), Richard Nixon sponsored a dinner in honor of the POWs at the White House and Jim stayed with us that weekend. After learning of his release, I had contacted the Air Force at Travis

AFB in California where the POWs were to land on their return to the United States.... Somehow the message got to him and he contacted me.

"Needless to say it was an extraordinary weekend for me. I did not know exactly what to expect. I had left the Air Force in 1970, six years after graduating from the Academy. I had spent a year in Vietnam (1967–68) and started law school right after I left the Air Force. I left Vietnam in June 1968—the contrast in our lives for the past six years could not have been more stark. So before the visit I was intrigued by Jim's POW experience and what effect it would have had on him. We had spoken by telephone perhaps once or twice before the visit, but they were relatively short conversations and quite general.

"My lasting impression of that visit was that Jim had not changed very much at all, to my very pleasant relief. As with all the other POWs, he had a bit of a time warp since he had been locked up and tortured for six years or so and was not that familiar with the events of the previous six years. However, I was very happy to note that his overall attitude and demeanor were very much unchanged. He was still the very together, even-tempered, pleasant, and very smart guy I had known six year years before. Outwardly, he was not particularly bitter about his experience nor that angry about his treatment as a POW. His attitude, as I remember it, was basically 'It's over and I am not going to allow it to determine the rest of my life. I am not going through life as a victim and former POW.' The lack of bitterness and, frankly, good humor was a bit startling to me at first because I just doubted that I could have acted that way.

"We discussed the 1972 election and how Richard Nixon had somehow managed to navigate through the Watergate break-in and still get elected. We also talked about many other events while he was a POW, including the great mistakes of the Vietnam War, which I have studied quite a bit. We also discussed whether he would stay in the Air Force, and he said he did not know yet, he was still thinking about that. He told me he would be going to an Air Force program, which he called "Re-Bluing," to re-acclimate to the Air Force. The next time we spoke about this, he said that "Re-Bluing" had turned out to be "De-Bluing," and he had decided to leave the Air Force and go to law school.

"In the spring of 2000, I visited with Jim in Spokane; I was living in Southern California then and doing some business in Seattle. On one trip I had arranged a detour to Spokane in the hope of seeing Jim and fortunately we were able to arrange that. What prompted that visit was a trip that my wife and I and one daughter had taken to Vietnam, which included a visit to Hanoi and the Hanoi Hilton, then operated by the Vietnamese government as a museum. It was not completely intact as during your father's imprisonment there, but much of it was still as it had been during its infamous time. So now I had actually seen the prison camp, the prison cells, the torture rooms and devices, all somewhat cosmeticized by the Vietnamese government to make it all look better than it had been. I took a fair number of photos on the visit to the prison camp, and I took the photos...with me when I visited Jim.

"During our visit, Jim remarked how the Vietnamese government had made various changes in the ensuing years—all to make it look better than it had been. In one room, for example, the Vietnamese had a wall of photos, including a photo of what looked like a rec room with a pool table—as if they were treating the POWs well. One of these photos on that wall showed Jim and one other POW at a pool table, and I had taken a photo of the photo because I thought that I recognized Jim in the Vietnamese photo. Jim could only smile and laugh at this, because he said yes he was in the Vietnamese photo, and he remembered when it had been taken, and he recognized the other POW in the picture. At the time the Vietnamese photo was taken, as I recall, Jim said the prison guards had finally relaxed the torture and mistreatment of the POWs, not to say they were treated decently, but the constant torture had generally ended, and perhaps the POWs were near release. He laughed about it and told me the Vietnamese photo was a posed shot, and he had not seen the final photo before. The POWs had decided by this time that they would go along with this sort of nonsense because it was just meaningless. The POWs only laughed at this sort of thing.

"The last time I talked with Jim was at an Academy reunion in 2004. I didn't know it was also goodbye. Fine man, good person, Jim Shively."

Bill Dickey, founder, president, and CEO, The Dermot Company, Inc., New York, NY

"I first met Jim when he was twelve and I was nine. He was our newspaper boy. I used to ask my parents if I could go to the door and pay the paper boy when he came to collect.... One year we went to Washington, D.C., for a POW reunion. I woke up to a strange noise in our hotel room. It was Jim, tapping on the wall to the POW in the room next to us!"

Nancy Banta Shively

"I moved six times in college. Every time, Dad showed up with his pickup and started hauling my furniture up and down stairs. He never complained or said a word about it.... The summer before he died, he was really sick from chemo and radiation. Even so, that didn't stop him from coming over to check on my roses."

Amy Shively Hawk

"Dad loved the snow—he would help us build great big snowmen. He'd also make snow angels with us, start snowball fights, and chase us around the house to put snow down our backs!...

"I remember all the summers at the lake. I would be dozing on a raft on the water, and Dad would quietly swim underneath my raft and tip me over....

"When I was in college, Dad would send me random cards in the mail, unsigned. I always knew they were from him, though!...

"After grad school, Dad flew down to Texas to help me drive back with all my stuff. He knew one of my pet peeves is when people order the same meal in a restaurant, so every time we stopped to eat we would discuss what each of us would order so that we could be sure we weren't ordering the same thing. And every time, after I placed my order, Dad would change his and order the same thing! I would get so irritated and he would just chuckle, every time."

Jane Shively Helbig

"I remember when Dad was teaching me how to drive a stick shift. Even though I stalled a hundred times and kept jerking us back and forth, he never got impatient with me....

"When Dad got a 1954 Plymouth with holes in the floor board, no back seat, and a rusty paint job, he would embarrass us by driving by cute boys' houses and honking the horn....

"Once when Amy, Nikki, and I went skiing...we dropped the car keys into the snow [from the chair lift]. Dad had to drive clear up to the mountain to leave us a spare key, but he didn't get mad or say a word about it."

Laura Shively Watson

"Dad coached our softball team when Laura and I were in fourth and fifth grades. The first lesson he taught us was to step up to the plate, adjust, and then spit....

"Dad read to us almost every night. Laura and I were only five or six years old, but he didn't read *Dr. Seuss*. He read *Treasure Island* or *Swiss Family Robinson*. Sometimes he would lie in bed with us while he read, and we would clean his ears.…

"I remember when I was little, I would wake up early in the morning and Dad would be the only one up. He would make some coffee for himself and some hot chocolate 'a little bit cold' for me, and we would sit quietly together. It was the best part of my day.

"A couple of Christmases when we were young, Dad drove us out to the woods in North Idaho to cut down a tree. The ones we picked out were always huge and way too big for our car. But he would somehow manage to get the tree on top of the car and drive all the way home—I'm sure he could barely see."

Nikki Shively Woodland

"On the Christmas Eve that Nikki and I got engaged, Nikki gave me a manila envelope to open on Christmas day, from Jim. I thought it would be a sentimental letter from him welcoming me to their family, and that he was just too shy to give it to me in person. Actually, it was a 5x7 photo of himself, wishing me a Merry Christmas."

Brett Woodland (Nikki's husband)

"Papa Jim always had time to make cookies with me. And we planted a huge sunflower patch—when I came over, we would run through it together."

Savanna Hawk

"Papa Jim made gingerbread houses with us every year, and he would let us eat all the frosting."

Cruise Hawk

NO HERO LIKE SHIVELY

"We are all looking for a hero. My dictionary says a 'hero' is a 'person of distinguished valor in danger, or fortitude in suffering,' or one 'who is honored because of exceptional service to mankind.' Jim was all that. Both in wartime and in civilian life, Jim showed guts, integrity, and toughness, was unblemished by arrogance or swagger, and leavened with kindness, calm patience, and understanding.

Jim Shively was a hero. I am grateful for the honor of having known such an extraordinary yet humble man. Jim, thank you for the gift of your service to all of us, both as a warrior who knew fear but never succumbed to it, and as a lawyer who never shrank back from doing the right thing no matter how hard that might have been. And thanks for your friendship."

Leslie Weatherhead, attorney, Spokane, WA

Acknowledgments

"Plans fail for lack of counsel, but with many advisers they succeed."

—Proverbs 15:22

I am indebted to an abundance of wise counselors. Among them I would like to thank:

Steve Becker, who met with Dad for six months to record his personal memoirs on tape. I don't know how you convinced him to do it, but we are all so glad you did! Steve, it was your foresight and perseverance that allowed me to write this book. Thank you for your persistence through recording problems, busy family schedules, and when Nancy forgot you were coming and came stumbling out of her bedroom at 7:00 a.m. and you gave her a fright. The Shively clan is forever indebted to you.

Senator John McCain for your genuine and very gracious contributions. Sir, this is about the best compliment I can give somebody: you remind me of Jim Shively.

Mike Burns and Joe Crecca, how can I thank you enough? This book wouldn't be the same without your stories about Dad, and your insight into his attitude and character during those long years of captivity. I know you were both special to him. Thank you for keeping his memory alive.

Bob Abbott and Gordon Jenkins, for your willingness to share about your adventures in combat training at Nellis (and Bob, your time spent in prison) with my Dad.

To Captain Mike McGrath, for your help in reviewing the chapters about the war and flying. Thank you for your patient correction, instruction, and encouragement!

Rolf Tangvald, your contribution to this book sums up the man Jim Shively was beautifully. Thank you for your devoted friendship to him and to our family.

Thank you to my husband, Steve, for making me listen to Dad's CDs when I didn't want to, and for encouraging me to write this book. Thank you for taking time to proof and edit, to offer ideas, and for just being your supportive self. I couldn't have written this book had it not been for your unwavering confidence that it was a worthwhile endeavor. I love you so much.

To Savanna and Cruise, who always manage to encourage me when I need it the very most—Savanna, thank you for making quesadillas so I could write. Cruise, thank you for rubbing my neck. I love you both so much!

To Shannon Eaglin, for praying me through. I love you, girlfriend!

To my cousin Chris Gilliland for searching through your mom's old scrapbooks and sending me material. Your assistance gave me details and photos I wouldn't have had otherwise. Thank you for your enthusiasm for this book, it means a lot to me!

With special thanks to my editor, Mary Beth Baker, for your thoughtful insights, and for pushing me. You made the book better.

Lastly, and mostly, to the men and women who serve our country—a heartfelt thank you for your courage. I esteem you highly, and also dedicate this memoir to the heroes whose stories have never been told, and to the families of those who didn't come back. Thank you for your tremendous sacrifice on our behalf.

As the *Veteran Tributes* website says,

Some People Dream the Dream...

Some People Live the Dream...

Some People Defend the Dream...

God Bless the Defenders...

...and God Bless America.

—Amy

Notes

CHAPTER 5: ONE MORE ROLL

1. First name changed to protect anonymity.
2. To see Captain James R. Shively's awards, visit the *Military Times* Hall of Valor, http://valor.militarytimes.com/recipient. php?recipientid=24736 (accessed June 22, 2016).

CHAPTER 6: SHOT DOWN

1. From a phone interview with Gordon Jenkins, February 1, 2015.

CHAPTER 8: DON'T LET THE BED BUGS BITE

1.   From a phone interview with Bob Abbott, January 17, 2015.

2.   All three of these examples of tapping communication are found in John H. Herd, *Operation Homecoming: 30th Anniversary 1973-2003* (Colorado Springs, CO: The United States Air Force Academy, 2003).

CHAPTER 9: MIND GAMES, EXPLOITATION, AND PROPAGANDA

1.   From a phone interview with Bob Abbott, January 17, 2015.

2.   Email correspondence with Joe Crecca, July 12, 2016.

3.   Additional sources about Doug Hegdahl: Bethanne Kelly Patrick, "Seaman Apprentice Douglas Hegdahl," Military. com, http://www.military.com/Content/ MoreContent?file=ML_hegdahl_bkp (accessed February 24, 2014); POW Network, "HEGDAHL, DOUGLAS BRENT," http://pownetwork.org/bios/h/h135.htm (accessed January 17, 2015).

CHAPTER 10: "A LITTLE SPARK OF HOPE"

1.   Ellen Ewing, *The Inland Register*, Spokane, WA.

2.   Excerpts of a letter from Jim found in Jeanette's scrapbook.

3.   From *The Spokane Daily Chronicle*, 1970. No author identified.

4.   From their website: "The League originated on the west coast in the late 1960s. Believing that the US Government's policy of

keeping a low profile on the POW/MIA issue while urging family members to refrain from publicly discussing the problem was unjustified, the wife of a ranking POW initiated a loosely organized movement that evolved into the National League of POW/MIA Families." http://www.pow-miafamilies.org/about-the-league/ (accessed September 29, 2014).

5.   J. Byrd Vissotzky, *The Other Side of the Coin* (San Francisco: Blurb Publishing, 1989), 76.

6.   Marie Bossio, quoted in "MIA Activist Dies; Memorial Planned," *Spokane Daily Chronicle*, October 1977.

7.   "POW Relatives Ending Long Trip," *The Daily Chronicle*, July 1, 1970. https://www.newspapers.com/newspage/25406071/.

CHAPTER 11: HANOI HANNAH, GYRO GEARLOOSE, AND LADIES' UNDERWEAR

1.   Joe Crecca, original essay for Jim Shively's Celebration of Life ceremony, March 2006.

2.   From an interview with Joe Crecca, March 25, 2014.

CHAPTER 12: ESCAPE AND REPERCUSSIONS: NEW LEVELS OF HELL

1.   Code of Conduct for Members of the United States Armed Forces III, http://www.au.af.mil/au/awc/awcgate/readings/code_of_conduct.htm (accessed June 29, 2016).

2. Biography of Ernest C. Brace, POW Network, http://www. pownetwork.org/bios/b/b603.htm (accessed January 23, 2016).

3. Biography of John Arthur Dramesi, POW Network, http:// www.pownetwork.org/bios/d/d059.htm (accessed April 1, 2014); Biography of Edwin Lee Atterberry, POW Network, http://www.pownetwork.org/bios/a/a044.htm (accessed January 19, 2015).

4. John M. McGrath, *Prisoner of War: Six Years in Hanoi* (Annapolis: Naval Institute Press, 1975), 44, 60, 64, 66, 84.

5. From a phone interview with Mike McGrath, October 23, 2014.

6. McGrath, *Prisoner of War*, 44, 60, 64, 66, 84.

7. Jim Dullenty, interview with Major Wesley D. Schierman and Captain James R. Shively, "Ex-City POWs tell of Red Tortures," *The Spokane Daily Chronicle*, 1973.

8. McGrath, *Prisoner of War*, 44, 60, 64, 66, 84; Craig Howes, *Voices of the Vietnam POWs: Witnesses to Their Fight* (New York: Oxford University Press, 1993), 105.

CHAPTER 13: CAMP FAITH

1. John S. McCain, "John McCain, Prisoner of War: A First-Person Account," *U.S. News & World Report*, January 28, 2008, http://www.usnews.com/news/articles/2008/01/28/ john-mccain-prisoner-of-war-a-first-person-account (accessed July 11, 2016).

2. "POW Prisons in North Vietnam," PBS Return with Honor, http://www.pbs.org/wgbh/amex/honor/sfeature/sf_prisons. html (accessed July 14, 2016).

3. Overall, camp accommodations generally improved across the board in the fall of 1969. No one knew why certain prisoners were selected for specific camps, except that the most senior ranking officials and "notable" prisoners (like John McCain) were kept in solitary longer than most.

4. Additional resources used for information regarding the Son Tây raid: William A. Guenon, Jr., *Secret and Dangerous; Night of the Son Tây POW Raid* (East Lowell: King Printing Company, Inc., 2002); Kennedy Hickman, Vietnam War: Raid on Son Tây http://militaryhistory.about.com/od/ vietnamwar/p/sontay.htm (accessed March 20, 2014.)

5. From an interview with Joe Crecca, March 25, 2014.

6. Todd Purdum, "Prisoner of Conscience," *Vanity Fair*, February 2007, http://www.vanityfair.com/news/2007/02/ mccain200702 (accessed July 14, 2016).

7. James Robinson Risner, "Robbie," http://www.pownetwork. org/bios/r/r039.htm (accessed June 16, 2016).

8. Story retold by Captain Guy Gruters, a prisoner who was present at the rebellion, during Amy's tour of the United States Air Force Academy, April 24, 2015; Colleen Slevin, "Former POW honored at Air Force Academy," www.pownetwork. org/bios/r/r039.htm (accessed June 4, 2015); Matt Schudel,

"Robinson Risner, Air Force ace and POW, dies at 88,"
Washington Post, http://www.washingtonpost.com/national/
robinson-risner-air-force-ace-and-pow-dies-at-88/2013/10/29/
ec759f3e-40ae-11e3-a624-41d661b0bb78_story.html
(accessed June 4, 2015).

9. Biography of Michael Durhen Christian, POW Network,
http://www.pownetwork.org/bios/c/c083.htm (accessed
January 27, 2016).

10. John S. McCain, "John McCain, Prisoner of War: A First-
Person Account," *U.S. News & World Report,* January 28,
2008, http://www.usnews.com/news/articles/2008/01/28/
john-mccain-prisoner-of-war-a-first-person-account?page=4
(accessed January 18, 2016).

11. From a phone interview with John McCain on October 20,
2015.

CHAPTER 15: OPERATION HOMECOMING

1. Quoted in Donna Miles, "Operation Homecoming for
Vietnam POWs Marks 40 Years," U.S. Department of
Defense, February 12, 2013, http://www.vietnamwar50th.
com/operation_homecoming_for_vietnam_pows_marks_40_
years/ (accessed June 16, 2016).

2. Laura M. Miller, "The Christmas Bombing of Hanoi Was
Justified (1 February 1973, Interview With Henry A.
Kissinger)," Dictionary of American History, The Gale Group

Inc., 2003, http://www.encyclopedia.com/
doc/1G2-3401804846.html (accessed June 16, 2016).

3.   "Paris Peace Accords signed," This Day in History, January
27, 1973, http://www.history.com/this-day-in-history/paris-
peace-accords-signed (accessed June 16, 2016).

4.   Jim Shively recording, CD 9, tracks 61–63.

5.   "Statistical Information about Fatal Casualties of the Vietnam
War," National Archives Military Records, http://www.
archives.gov/research/military/vietnam-war/casualty-statistics.
html (accessed January 20, 2015); Defense POW/MIA
Accounting Agency, Vietnam War, http://www.dpaa.mil/Our-
Missing/Vietnam-War/Vietnam-War-POW-MIA-List/
(accessed July 18, 2016); "Operation Homecoming for
Vietnam POWs marks 40 years," U.S. Air Force, February 12,
2013, http://www.af.mil/News/ArticleDisplay/tabid/223/
Article/109716/operation-homecoming-for-vietnam-pows-
marks-40-years.aspx (accessed July 18, 2016).

CHAPTER 16: RETURN TO FREEDOM

1.   Air Force Major General Ed Mechenbier, quoted in Donna
Miles, "Operation Homecoming for Vietnam POWs Marks
40 Years," U.S. Department of Defense, February 12, 2013,
http://www.vietnamwar50th.com/operation_homecoming_
for_vietnam_pows_marks_40_years/ (accessed July 18, 2016).

2.   Air Force Captain Larry Chesley, quoted in Donna Miles,
"Operation Homecoming for Vietnam POWs Marks 40

Years," U.S. Department of Defense, February 12, 2013, http://www.vietnamwar50th.com/operation_homecoming_ for_vietnam_pows_marks_40_years/ (accessed July 18, 2016).

3. Hal Drake, "Tears, cheers, love greet POWs at Clark," *Stars and Stripes,* December 11, 1973, http://www.stripes.com/ news/pacific/tears-cheers-love-greet-pows-at-clark-1.163263 (accessed July 12, 2016).

4. Carol Bates Brown, "History of the POW/MIA Bracelet," The Vietnam Veterans Memorial, The Wall-USA, http://www. thewall-usa.com/bracelet.asp (accessed June 16, 2016); "POW Bracelets," The National Museum of American History, http:// americanhistory.si.edu/collections/search/object/ nmah_1273063 (accessed July 21, 2016).

5. Hal Drake, "Tears, cheers, love greet POWs at Clark."

6. Jim Dullenty, "Family Greets Capt. Shively," the *Spokane Daily Chronicle,* February 21, 1973; "800 Welcome 18 Ex-Prisoners As They Land at Travis Base," *The Oregonian,* February 21, 1973.

7. "Newly Freed Shively Sees Family Again," *The Spokesman-Review,* February 21, 1973.

8. From a phone interview with Patsy Chambers, October 4, 2014.

CHAPTER 17: LIFE IN THE SPOTLIGHT

1. Phone interview with Bob Banta, September 28, 2014.

2. Richard Nixon, "Remarks at a Reception for Returned Prisoners of War," May 24, 1973, The American Presidency, http://www.presidency.ucsb.edu/ws/?pid=3856 (accessed June 28, 2016). "POWs Celebrate at 40th Anniversary Homecoming Dinner," Richard Nixon Foundation, http:// nixonfoundation.org/2013/05/webcast-tonight-at-6pmpt9pmet-pow-reunion-dinner/ (accessed June 28, 2016).

3. Douglas Martin, "Ernest Brace, Civilian Pilot Held as P.O.W. in Vietnam, Dies at 83," *New York Times*, December 8, 2014, http://www.nytimes.com/2014/12/09/us/ernest-brace-civilian-pilot-held-as-pow-in-vietnam-dies-at-83.html (accessed January 23, 2016).

4. Gayle Kelley, "The President Hosts Ex- POWs," *Standard-Times*, May 1973.

5. Major Robert W. Hunter, "White House Party For The POWs," *Air Force Magazine*, July 1973, 81.

CHAPTER 18: DON'T SWEAT THE SMALL STUFF

1. Bill Morlin, "Ex- POW Shively dies at 63," *The Spokesman-Review*, February 23, 2006, http://www.armedpolitesociety.com/index.php?topic=2602.0;wap2 (accessed October 10, 2014).

2. Phone interview with Bob Banta, September 28, 2014.

3. Jerry Hughes, "Former POW Shively A Lasting Inspiration," *The Spokesman-Review*, February 25, 2006.

4. Wade Evans, "No Feast," *Spokane Chronicle*, November 26, 1981.

5. Morlin, "Ex-POW Shively dies at 63."

6. Bill Morlin, "Lost in Fire, Ex-POWs Medals Replaced," *The Spokesman-Review*, March 24, 1992, https://news.google.com/newspapers?nid=1314&dat=19920324&id=509XAAAA IBAJ&sjid=O_ADAAAAIBAJ&pg=1938,2650327&hl=en.

7. Jim Shively, journal entry September 26, 1991.

CHAPTER 19: BECAUSE YOU CANNOT HATE AND LIVE

1. Jeff Bauer, "Ex-Vietnam POW tells North Pines crowd there is no room for failure," *Spokane Valley Herald*.

2. Jim Shively, quoted in Michael Murphey, "Bobby Johnston will be OK, but what about the rest of us?" *Spokane Chronicle*, January 1983.

3. Ken Sands, "Kidnapper Johnston Won't Go To Jail," *Spokesman-Review*, April 9, 1983.

4. Jim Shively, quoted in Jim Spoerhase, "Vet Shocked by Kidnap Conviction," *Spokane Chronicle*, January 17, 1983.

5. Jim Shively, quoted in Murphey, "Bobby Johnston will be ok, but what about the rest of us?"

6. Ibid.

7. Sands, "Kidnapper Johnston Won't Go To Jail."

CHAPTER 20: THE LAST BATTLE

1. Jim Shively, journal entry September 26, 1991.

2. Phone interview with Mike Burns, January 19, 2015.
3. March 3, 2006.

Index